Two Great Plays by

W. H. AUDEN and

CHRISTOPHER ISHERWOOD

Two Great Plays by

W. H. AUDEN AND

CHRISTOPHER ISHERWOOD

The Dog Beneath the Skin

The Ascent of F6

VINTAGE BOOKS

A DIVISION OF RANDOM HOUSE

New York

The Dog Beneath the Skin

Or, Where Is Francis?

67-36262

TO ROBERT MOODY

Boy with lancet, speech or gun
  Among the dangerous ruins, learn
From each devastated organ
  The power of the genteel dragon.

Dramatis Personae

Principal Characters

The Vicar of Pressan Ambo
General Hotham
Mrs. Hotham, his wife
Miss Iris Crewe, of Honeypot Hall
Sir Francis Crewe, Bart: her brother
Alan Norman
First Journalist (*The Evening Moon*)
Second Journalist (*The Thunderbolt*)

Minor Characters

Curate
Mildred Luce
H.M. The King of Ostnia
H.M. The Queen of Ostnia
Grabstein, a Financier
Destructive Desmond

Sorbo Lamb
Chimp Eagle
Sir William Spurgeon, the Surgeon
Madame Bubbi

Others

Bus Conductor
Hotel Porter
Village Chemist
Scout-Master
Master of Ceremonies
Poet
Cabaret Announcer
Head Waiter
Art Expert
Hotel Manager
Barman
Chorus Girls
Courtiers
Diners

Doctors
Dressers
Invalids
Lunatics
Nurses
Police
Priests
Procurers
Prostitutes
Students
Waiters
Villagers
Two Lovers
Two Touts

Chorus

The Summer holds: upon its glittering lake
Lie Europe and the islands; many rivers
Wrinkling its surface like a ploughman's palm.
Under the bellies of the grazing horses
On the far side of posts and bridges
The vigorous shadows dwindle; nothing wavers.
Calm at this moment the Dutch sea so shallow
That sunk St. Pauls would ever show its golden cross
And still the deep water that divides us still from Norway.
We would show you at first an English village: You shall
    choose its location
Wherever your heart directs you most longingly to look; you
    are loving towards it:
Whether north to Scots Gap and Bellingham where the black
    rams defy the panting engine:
Or west to the Welsh Marches; to the lilting speech and the ma-
    gicians' faces:
Wherever you were a child or had your first affair
There it stands amidst your darling scenery:
A parish bounded by the wreckers' cliff; or meadows where
    browse the Shorthorn and the maplike Frisian
As at Trent Junction where the Soar comes gliding; out of
    green Leicestershire to swell the ampler current.

Hiker with sunburn blisters on your office pallor,
Cross-country champion with corks in your hands,
When you have eaten your sandwich, your salt and your apple,
When you have begged your glass of milk from the ill-kept
    farm,
What is it you see?

I see barns falling, fences broken,
Pasture not ploughland, weeds not wheat.
The great houses remain but only half are inhabited,
Dusty the gunrooms and the stable clocks stationary.
Some have been turned into prep-schools where the diet is in
    the hands of an experienced matron,
Others into club-houses for the golf-bore and the top-hole.
Those who sang in the inns at evening have departed; they saw
    their hope in another country,

Their children have entered the service of the suburban areas;
    they have become typists, mannequins and factory opera-
    tives; they desired a different rhythm of life.
But their places are taken by another population, with views
    about nature,
Brought in charabanc and saloon along arterial roads;
Tourists to whom the Tudor cafés
Offer Bovril and buns upon Breton ware
With leather work as a sideline: Filling stations
Supplying petrol from rustic pumps.
Those who fancy themselves as foxes or desire a special setting
    for spooning
Erect their villas at the right places,
Airtight, lighted, elaborately warmed;
And nervous people who will never marry
Live upon dividends in the old-world cottages
With an animal for friend or a volume of memoirs.
Man is changed by his living; but not fast enough.
His concern to-day is for that which yesterday did not occur.
In the hour of the Blue Bird and the Bristol Bomber, his
    thoughts are appropriate to the years of the Penny Far-
    thing:
He tosses at night who at noonday found no truth.

Stand aside now: The play is beginning
In the village of which we have spoken; called Pressan Ambo:
Here too corruption spreads its peculiar and emphatic odours
And Life lurks, evil, out of its epoch.

LEADER OF SEMI-CHORUS I
        The young men in Pressan to-night
            Toss on their beds
        Their pillows do not comfort
            Their uneasy heads.
        The lot that decides their fate
            Is cast to-morrow,
        One must depart and face
            Danger and sorrow.

VOICES   Is it me? Is it me? Is it . . . me?

LEADER OF SEMI-CHORUS II
        Look in your heart and see:
            There lies the answer.
        Though the heart like a clever
            Conjuror or dancer

Deceive you often into many
    A curious sleight
And motives like stowaways
    Are found too late.

VOICES   What shall he do, whose heart
    Chooses to depart?

LEADER OF SEMI-CHORUS I
    He shall against his peace
        Feel his heart harden,
    Envy the heavy birds
        At home in a garden.
    For walk he must the empty
        Selfish journey
    Between the needless risk
        And the endless safety.

VOICES   Will he safe and sound
    Return to his own ground?

LEADER OF SEMI-CHORUS II
    Clouds and lions stand
        Before him dangerous
    And the hostility of dreams.
        Oh let him honour us
    Lest he should be ashamed
        In the hour of crisis,
    In the valleys of corrosion
        Tarnish his brightness.

VOICES   Who are you, whose speech
    Sounds far out of reach?

BOTH LEADERS (*singing*)
    You are the town and we are the clock.
    We are the guardians of the gate in the rock.
        The Two.
    On your left and on your right
    In the day and in the night,
        We are watching you.

    Wiser not to ask just what has occurred
    To them who disobeyed our word;
        To those
    We were the whirlpool, we were the reef,
    We were the formal nightmare, grief
        And the unlucky rose.

Climb up the crane, learn the sailor's words
When the ships from the islands laden with birds
 Come in.
Tell your stories of fishing and other men's wives:
The expansive moments of constricted lives
 In the lighted inn.
But do not imagine we do not know
Nor that what you hide with such care won't show
 At a glance.
Nothing is done, nothing is said,
But don't make the mistake of believing us dead:
 I shouldn't dance.

We're afraid in that case you'll have a fall.
We've been watching you over the garden wall
 For hours.
The sky is darkening like a stain,
Something is going to fall like rain
 And it won't be flowers.

When the green field comes off like a lid
Revealing what was much better hid:
 Unpleasant.
And look, behind you without a sound
The woods have come up and are standing round
 In deadly crescent.

The bolt is sliding in its groove,
Outside the window is the black removers van
And now with sudden swift emergence
Come the woman in dark glasses and the humpbacked
  surgeons
 And the scissor man.

This might happen any day
So be careful what you say
 Or do.
Be clean, be tidy, oil the lock,
Trim the garden, wind the clock,
 Remember the Two.

Act One

Scene 1

(The garden of the Vicarage at Pressan Ambo. The scene suggests the setting of a pre-war musical comedy. The stage is crowded with villagers of all classes, who promenade to the strains of a distant band. The characters, as they pass in turn along the footlights, address the audience)

VICAR	Here come I, the Vicar good
	Of Pressan Ambo, it's understood;
	    Within this parish border
	I labour to expound the truth
	To train the tender plant of Youth
	    And guard the moral order.

CHORUS	With troops of scouts for village louts And preaching zest he does his best To guard the moral order.
GENERAL	General Hotham is my name. At Tatra Lakes I won my fame, I took the Spanish Lion. In Pressan now my home I've made And rule my house like a brigade With discipline of iron.
CHORUS	Side by side his peacocks stride: He rules them all at Conyers Hall With discipline of iron.
GENERAL'S WIFE	
	Woman, though weak, must do her part And I who keep the General's heart Know well our island story And do my utmost to advance

In India, Russia, Finland, France,
    The just and English glory.

CHORUS   With subtle wile and female smile,
    With speech and vote she will promote
        The just and English glory.

IRIS   And here am I, Miss Iris Crewe,
    I live in Pressan Ambo too,
        The prize at village dances.
    From Honeypot Hall, the haunt of doves,
    In my blue Daimler and white gloves
        I come to take your glances.

CHORUS   With nose and ear and mouth and hair
    With fur and hat and things like that
        She takes our loving glances.

VICAR (*to* CHOIRBOYS)
    Well, Ernie, how's your mother? Good.
    I hope you're behaving as you should?
    Jerry, you've got a dirty face;
    Go and wash. Then we'll have a race.

1ST VILLAGER   Brazen! I should think she is!
    She doesn't care who sees them kiss,
    Can't even trouble to draw the blind.
    She's a trollop to my mind.

2ND V.   The brooder's really excellent.
    I rear now 98 per cent.
    I have a new batch out to-day:
    Leghorns, for I find they pay.

3RD V.   I shan't mind if they choose me.
    There's lots of places I want to see:
    Paris, Vienna, Berlin, Rome.
    I shouldn't be sorry to leave the home.

4TH V.   Roll the pieces then in flour
    And stew them for at least an hour,
    Put some nutmeg in the pot
    Garnish with parsley and serve hot.

3RD V.   Perhaps they will, you never know;
    What will you do if you have to go?

2ND V.   There's money to be made in sheep;
    Only you mustn't go to sleep.

4TH V.   A glass of stout before the meal
    Is always a good thing, I feel.

VICAR (*starting the race*)
              Are we ready? Now Chubb, don't cheat!
              Behind the line and touch your feet.

1ST V.   No wonder they have had a quarrel,
              The Continent is so immoral.

4TH V.   Be very careful how you add the salt.

1ST V.   Well, anyway, it's not his fault.

3RD V.   After eight years, it seems absurd.

VICAR   Ernie first, Chubb second, Pring third.

1ST V.   That dance at least should have opened his eyes.

2ND V.   Roger's heifer won first prize.

1ST V.   She's carrying on with Fred.

VICAR   Run up!
              You'll beat him yet!

4TH V.   This cider-cup
              Is good.

2ND V.   Ten shillings profit on the porks.

3RD V.   Chimp Eagle.

4TH V.   Recipe from wireless talks.

1ST V.   Someone ought to.

2ND V.   Well, we can't complain.

VICAR   Caught you, my lad!

3RD V.   He'll be lost again.

1ST V.   You saw her.

VICAR   Clever boy!

2ND V.   It's sold.

4TH V.   Taste it.

3RD V.   Choose someone.

1ST V.   He's too old.

2ND V.   Barley.

3RD V.   The Choice.

VICAR   Your legs.

1ST V.   Her name.

VICAR   Jolly!

4TH V.   Roasted.

3RD V.   The Hall.

1ST V.   The shame.

4TH V.   Ursula.

3RD V.   Saxifrage.

2ND V.   Wyandottes.

VICAR   Game!

2ND V.   He didn't!

1ST V.   She did!

VICAR   We must.

3RD V.   Yes.

4TH V.   No.

VOICES   (*in crescendo*)
          Good.
              Bad.
                  Poor.
                      Rich.
                          White.
                              Black.
                                  High.
                                      Low.
          Touch.
              Find.
                  Pay.
                      Eat.
                          Weep.
                              Hurt.
                                  Come.
                                      Go.
          Boy.
              Tea.
                  Lamb.
                      Crewe.
                          Shame.
                              Price.
                                  O!

(*The hubbub is interrupted by the* VICAR, *who mounts on to
a chair and begins ringing a Stationmaster's bell. Everybody
is silent*)

VICAR   Ladies and Gentlemen. I think that there
Are several strangers to Pressan here.
On your behalf I give them greeting
And will explain the purpose of our meeting:
The ancient family of Crewe
(It may perhaps be known to you)
For generations owned the land,
The farms, the fields on which we stand.
Sir Bingham Crewe, who was the last,
(God rest his soul, for he has passed)
We touched our hats to, had a son,
A handsome lad, his only one,
Called Francis, who was to succeed him.
Would he were here! We badly need him.
They quarrelled, I am sad to say,
And so, ten years ago to-day,
Young Francis packed and ran away
Leaving behind him no address.
Where he has gone, we cannot guess;
For since that day no news at all
Of where he is has reached the Hall.
In fact, we do not even know
If he be living still or no.

Sir Bingham died eight years ago,
Francis his heir being missing still,
And left these clauses in his will:
Each year, his villages in turn
Should choose by lottery a man
To find Sir Francis if he can:
Further, he promised half his land,
And Iris his daughter adds her hand
In marriage to the lucky one
Who comes home with his only son.

This year is Pressan's turn to choose.
Oh may this year bring the good news!

A VILLAGER (*sings*)
It seems such ages since the Master's son
      Went away.
He left his books, his clothes, his boots, his
      car, his gun
   On that dreadful summer's day.
He vanished suddenly without a single
   word of warning:

Left us alone to make our moan;
He left us mourning.

CHORUS   Why has Fate been blind to our tears?
Why has she been so unkind to our fears?
Who shall we send this time who shall look
           for him,
   Search every corner and cranny and nook
           for him?
     It may be you the lot will fall upon,
     It may be me the lot will fall upon
           To guide back
           With pride back
       Our young heir Sir Francis Crewe!

VILLAGER   Without his face we don't know what to do,
           We're undone.
He was a beauty with a sense of duty, too,
           He was our brother and our son.
His wit, his charm, his strength, his manners,
           his modesty and his virtue
       Were we to tell, your contrast, well,
       With him would hurt you.

CHORUS   Why has Fate . . . etc.

CURATE (*to the* VICAR)   The names have all come in.
           We're ready to begin.

VICAR   Excellent. Excellent.
   (*A top hat is passed to him by the* POLICE SERGEANT)
                 Do you swear
       That all the names are written here
       Of every man in this village alive,
       Unmarried and over twenty-five?

SERGEANT   I swear it.

VICAR   Miss Iris Crewe.
   (IRIS *comes forward*)
                 Iris Crewe, are you willing now
       In the presence of these people to make
           your vow?

IRIS   I am.

VICAR (IRIS *repeats each phrase after him*)
       I, Iris Crewe, do solemnly swear
       In the presence of these people here,

> That I will be the wedded wife
> To love and cherish all my life
> Of him, whoever he may be,
> Who brings my brother back to me.

VICAR   Read the names of those we sent
> Who failed to do the thing they meant.

SERGEANT   Nobby Sollers.
> Sorbo Lamb.
> Frenchie Joe.
> Chimp Eagle.
> The Midget.
> Muffin Todd.
> Nicky Peterson.

(*The* VICAR's *eyes are bound with a handkerchief. He stirs the hat and draws, saying:*)
> Divvy Divvy Divvy Divvy Divvy Divvy Di
> Divvy Divvy Divvy Divvy Divvy Divvy Di.
>> Swans in the air. Swans in the air.
>> Let the chosen one appear!

CURATE   (*taking paper from him and reading*)
> Alan Norman.

(*A short burst of cheering*)

VICAR   (*removing the bandage*)   Alan Norman.
(ALAN *comes forward and kneels*)
>> Alan Norman, will you go
> Cross any border in sand or snow,
> Will you do whatever may be needful
> Though people and customs both be hateful,
> When mind and members go opposite way,
> Watching wake folding long on sea;
> Will you remain a passenger still
> Nor desperate plunge for home?

ALAN   I will.

VICAR   (*producing a bag*)   Here is what the trustees give
> That as you journey you may live:
> Five hundred pounds; no more no less.
> May it help you to success.

(ALAN *accepts the bag and bows*)
> Let us stand a moment in silent prayer.

(*All the men present remove their hats. The* DOG *enters and begins sniffing about. People surreptitiously kick it or pat it, but it refuses to stay quiet*)

SEMI-CHORUS I   Enter with him
These legends, love,
For him assume
Each diverse form
As legend simple
As legend queer
That he may do
What these require
Be, love, like him
To legend true.

SEMI-CHORUS II   When he to ease
His heart's disease
Must cross in sorrow
Corrosive seas
As dolphin go,
As cunning fox
Guide through the rocks,
Tell in his ear
The common phrase
Required to please
The guardians there.
And when across
The livid marsh
Big birds pursue
Again be true
Between his thighs
As pony rise
As swift as wind
Bear him away
Till cries and they
Are left behind.

CHORUS   But when at last
These dangers past
His grown desire
Of legends tire
O then, love, standing
At legends' ending,
Claim your reward
Submit your neck
To the ungrateful stroke
Of his reluctant sword
That starting back
His eyes may look
Amazed as you

> Find what he wanted
> Is faithful too
> But disenchanted
> Your simplest love.

VICAR   Well, Alan, let me congratulate
> You first and then ourselves and Fate.
> We couldn't have chosen a better man.
> If you can't succeed, then no one can.

(*Sees* DOG)

> There's that dog again! I'm blest!
> I thought I'd lost him like the rest.
> George, George! Good dog! Come here!
> Walk George, walk.

(*He whistles. The* DOG *runs away*)

> That's queer!

(*Everybody looks at the* DOG, *who walks round, snuffling and refusing advances*)

GENERAL   If you ask me, I shouldn't wonder if that dog wasn't sickening for the rabies. Most extraordinary animal I ever came across. Turns up on your doorstep one morning with his tongue hanging out, like the prodigal son; lets you feed him, slobber over him, pet him, makes himself quite at home. In an hour or two he's one of the family. And then, after a week or a fortnight, he'll be off again, cool as you please. Doesn't know you if you meet him in the street. And he's played the same trick on all of us. Confounded ungrateful brute! It's his mongrel blood, of course. No loyalty; no proper feeling. Though I'm bound to say, while he was with me he was the best gun-dog I ever had. (*To* DOG) Come here, sir. Heel, sir. Heel!!

(*The* DOG *regards the* GENERAL *for a moment with an almost human contempt. Then it continues its snuffling*)

VILLAGERS   Isn't he sweet?
> Here is some meat.
> If he were to choose
> Me, I couldn't refuse.
> If he'd come to me
> I'd give him cake for tea.

(*The* DOG *reaches* ALAN *and begins to fawn upon him and wag its tail*)

VILLAGERS   Oh look! He's chosen you!
> What are you going to do?

ALAN   I'll take him too.

ALL   You must name him anew.

ALAN   For luck I'll call him Francis.

ALL   Oh, look how he prances!

BUS CONDUCTOR   The village bus is about to start
             Those who are coming prepare to depart.

VICAR (*giving a small parcel to* ALAN)
             Here is a tin of Church of England Mixture
             Just to show you that our friendship is a fixture.
             Smoke it while you are a vagrant
             And may it keep our memory fragrant.

CURATE   I have a little present here,
             It's just some trustworthy underwear.
             May its high-grade Botany wool
             Keep you warm and keep you cool.

VILLAGE CHEMIST
             Here is some Victo for the nerves, in case
             The Man Next Door should take your place.

A SCOUTMASTER   Here is a Kron watch; like a wife
             To keep exact time all your life,
             Generously designed to offer beauty
             And like an Englishman to do its duty.
             A nameless watch is scarcely better
             Than an anonymous letter.
             (*During these speeches, the* GENERAL *has been having a
             whispered consultation with his* WIFE)

GENERAL'S WIFE   Oh *no,* dear! I'm sure ten shillings would be
                 ample.

GENERAL (*advancing pompously to* ALAN)
             Ahem! Ahem!
             (*He gives money with the air of tipping a porter*)
             Don't disgrace Pressan Ambo, my boy.

ALAN   Rather not, sir! Thanks awfully, sir!

IRIS   Alan dearest, we must part
             But keep this photo near your heart,
             Wherever you go, by land or sea,
             Look on this and think of me:
             For whatever you must do
             My thoughts are always with you too.

ALAN   Iris, give me a parting kiss
             In promise of our future bliss.

IRIS   Gladly, Alan, I give you this.
  (*Embrace*)

VOICES   Oh dear, it's beginning to rain!
          You ought to weed it.
          The farmers need it.
          Mummy, I've got a pain.

ALL   Speech! Speech!

ALAN   You've been so ripping and kind
          It puts all words out of my mind,
          But if there's anything I can do,
          Ladies and Gentlemen, for you. . . .

MILDRED LUCE (*suddenly appearing*)   Yes!
          Set off for Germany and shoot them all!
          Poison the wells, till her people drink the sea
          And perish howling. Strew all her fields
          With arsenic, leave a land whose crops
          Would starve the unparticular hyena!
          But you are young and it is useless
          To look to Youth. In the November Silence
          I have heard more shuffling every year,
          Seen more of the up-to-date young man there
                    Waiting
          Impatient in the crowd to catch a train
          And shake a German gently by the hand.
          I had two sons as tall as you:
          A German sniper shot them both.
          They crawled to me across the floor;
          I put their earliest prattle in a book.
          A German sniper shot them both.
          I saw them win prizes at their prep-school sports,
          I had their friends at half-term out to tea.
          A German sniper shot them both.
          I heard their voices alter as they grew
          Shyer of me and more like men.
  (*Taking out a large watch*)
          O Ticker, Ticker, they are dead
          As the Grimaldi infants.
          Justice has gone a summer cruise and let
          Her mansion to a madman. Say something,
          Ticker. Nothing. Nothing. I protest.

VICAR   Mildred dear, go home and rest
          And calm yourself. That will be best.
  (*Sounds of a motor-horn*)

BUS-CONDUCTOR   The bus is leaving in a minute:
　　　　　　　　Those who are coming must step in it.

ALAN AND CHORUS   Now $\left\{ \begin{array}{c} I \\ we \end{array} \right\}$ must part
　　　　　　It's time to start
　　　　　　With tears in $\left\{ \begin{array}{c} my \\ our \end{array} \right\}$ eyes $\left\{ \begin{array}{c} I \\ we \end{array} \right\}$ say goodbyes.
　　　　　　Success be with you and satisfaction
　　　　　　We wish to you in your every action.
　　　　　　In July and December $\left\{ \begin{array}{c} I \\ we \end{array} \right\}$ will remember you!

(ALAN *goes out*. ALL *wave handkerchiefs and hands*)

CURTAIN

Chorus

Salmon leaping the ladder, eel in damp grass, the mole and the
　　tiercel:
Such images of travel do not apply.
Our impulses are unseasonal and image-ridden: our trifling dis-
　　turbances are without crisis.
Our sex and our sorrow are ever about us, like the sultriness of
　　a summer
As about our hero on his human journey,
Crossing a channel: on sea in steamer
For Ostnia and Westland, in post-war Europe.

　　　　Creatures of air and darkness, from this hour
　　　　　　Put and keep our friend in power.
　　　　Let not the reckless heavenly riders
　　　　　　Treat him and us as rank outsiders.

　　　　From the accosting sickness and
　　　　　　Love's fascinating biassed hand,
　　　　The lovely grievance and the false address,
　　　　　　From con-man and coiner protect and bless.

Scene II

(*The saloon of a Channel steamer. Behind the bar, the* BAR-MAN *is polishing glasses. The two* JOURNALISTS *are seated, drinking. A small piano against the wall*)

1ST JOURNALIST   The Old Man sent for me before I left. Wants me to get the low-down on the Dripping Merger. Officially, I'm covering the Danube floods.

2ND J.   I saw Timmy last night. He's just back from the Carpathians. Tight as usual. He had all the dope about the Army Contracts trial. Some kid, Timmy.

1ST J.   I heard a bit about that from Gus. Blankets, wasn't it?

2ND J.   Blankets nothing! Why, man, it was tarpaulin!

1ST J.   You've got it wrong, old horse. Gus said five million blankets.

2ND J.   Six million. . . .

1ST J.   Gus swears it was five.

2ND J.   To Hell with Gus. As I was saying, these tarpaulins. . . .

1ST J.   My dear old fish, Gus had it from the War Minister himself. . . . "Blankets," he said. . . .

2ND J.   Boy, you give me a pain. The whole *beauty* of the thing was that they were tarpaulins, don't you see . . . ?
(*Enter* ALAN *and the* DOG. *The* JOURNALISTS *stop arguing and watch him.* ALAN *crosses the stage to the bar*)

ALAN   (*diffidently*)   A double whisky, please: And a glass of milk.

BARMAN   Certainly, sir.

ALAN   (*embarrassed*)   And I wonder if you'd mind putting the whisky in a bowl?

BARMAN   (*puzzled*)   A bowl, sir?

ALAN   It's for my dog, you see.
(*The* BARMAN *winks at the* JOURNALISTS. 1ST JOURNALIST *taps his head significantly.* 2ND JOURNALIST *nods agreement*)

BARMAN (*suavely*) Ah, to be sure, sir.

ALAN (*confidentially*) Did *you* ever hear of a dog drinking whisky before? *I* never did. I only found it out as we were coming down on the train. An old gent in our compartment had ordered a bottle, and, before you could say Jack Robinson, Francis had swallowed the lot!

BARMAN Most remarkable, sir. Water or soda, sir?
(*The* DOG *begins howling*)

ALAN Rather not! He always drinks it neat, don't you, Francis, old boy? (*The* DOG *wags its tail*) Perhaps we'd better say two double whiskies. It doesn't look much when you pour it into a bowl, does it? (*The* BARMAN *adds the whiskies.* ALAN *gives the bowl to the* DOG, *who laps eagerly*) You see? And he won't touch anything else. I've tried him with tea, coffee, cocoa, lemonade, beer, wine, everything you can think of . . . I'm afraid I'm going to find it rather expensive.
(*He sighs and sips his glass of milk*)

BARMAN You're teetotal yourself, I see, sir?

ALAN (*blushing*) Ha ha! You mustn't think I've given it up on moral grounds, or any rot of that sort. . . . The fact is, I only started yesterday. You see, I want to keep a clear head all the time. I've got some rather difficult business to settle.

BARMAN Indeed, sir?

ALAN Yes. I'm looking for someone. Perhaps you might be able to help me? Have you been working on this boat for long?

BARMAN A matter of fifteen years, sir.

ALAN Why, that's splendid! Then you're almost sure to have seen him. His name's Francis Crewe.

BARMAN Can't say that I seem to recall it, sir. Can you describe him at all?

ALAN Well, no. I'm afraid I can't do that. You see, he left home ten years ago and that was before we came to live in the village. Here's the only photograph they'd got of him. It isn't much use. It was taken when he was six months old.

BARMAN (*examining photo*) Bless his little heart! Why, he's the spit and image of what my Jacky used to be. And now he can lift his poor old father up with one arm. In the marines, is my Jacky. Getting married next month.

ALAN   I'm getting married too, soon. At least, I hope I am. Look, here's a picture of my fiancée. What do you think of her? Isn't she a ripper?

BARMAN   I congratulate you, sir.
(*The* DOG *growls*)

ALAN   Shut up, Francis, you old silly! (*To* BARMAN) It's an extraordinary thing: Whenever I show that photograph of Iris to anybody, he begins to growl. Just as though he were jealous. . . . Here, Francis. Shake a paw.
(*The* DOG *turns away*)

BARMAN   You see, sir, he's offended. (*Slily*) If you were to offer him another whisky, he'd be ready to make it up, I'm sure.

ALAN   (*reluctantly*)   All right, if you think so.
(*The* DOG *immediately turns round and begins barking and licking* ALAN'S *hand*)

BARMAN   What did I tell you, sir? Nobody can resist a good whisky.
(*He looks pointedly at the bottle*)

ALAN   I say, I'm most awfully sorry. I ought to have asked you if you'd have a drink, too.

BARMAN   Well, sir: Since you're so pressing.

ALAN   By the way, have you ever been to Ostnia?

BARMAN   Can't say I have, sir. My brother was waiter at the Grand Hotel in the capital at one time.

ALAN   Do you know if it's the sort of country where people are likely to get lost?

BARMAN   I'm not sure I take your meaning, sir.

ALAN   You see, I thought of beginning my search there. I didn't know where to start, so I just shut my eyes and put my finger on the map.

BARMAN   And a very good idea too, sir. Your health, sir.
(*They touch glasses. The* DOG *lifts up the bowl in its paws and touches* ALAN'S *glass. They all drink*)

1ST J.   What do you make of him?

2ND J.   Queer sort of card. Might be a munitions agent.

1ST J.   Doubt it. I know most of them by sight.

2ND J.   Or in the dope traffic.

1st j.   Hasn't got a scarab ring.

2nd j.   A white slaver?

1st j.   They generally wear spats.

2nd j.   Secret Service, maybe.

1st j.   With that tie? Not on your life!

2nd j.   There's something phony about him, anyhow. Come on, let's get acquainted. There'll be a story in it, you bet. (*Loudly, to* ALAN) Pardon me, sir. Did I hear you saying just now that you were travelling to Ostnia?

ALAN Why, yes. Can you tell me anything about it? I'd be ever so grateful.

1st j.   Can we? I should say so! My colleague here knows Ostnia like the inside of his hat.

2nd j.   Pretty little country, Ostnia. Biggest national debt and lowest birth-rate in Europe. Half the budget goes into frontier forts, which are no more use than a headache because the contractor's a crook. The railways are so old they aren't safe, the mines are mostly flooded and the factories do nothing but catch fire. The Commander-in-Chief is no better than a bandit: He makes all the big stores pay for protection. The Archbishop spends his time copying naval plans for the Westland Intelligence Bureau. And meanwhile, the peasants die of typhus. Believe me, kid, it's God's own land.

ALAN I say! It must be awfully dangerous there, isn't it?

1st j.   Not for tourists. They only see the mountains and the Renaissance Palace. . . . Of course, when you get behind the scenes, you're liable to be bumped off if you don't watch out.

ALAN I shall have to be careful, then. You see, I'm looking for someone named Francis Crewe. . . .

2nd j.   See here, boy. You can keep that blue-eyed stuff for the others. You don't have to do it on us. We're not inquisitive.

1st j.   Don't worry. We'll show you the ropes.

2nd j.   Maybe we should introduce ourselves. I'm on the *Thunderbolt*.

1st j.   And I'm the live wire of the *Evening Moon*.

ALAN (*shaking hands*) I say! Are you really? I've always
wanted to meet some proper writers. (*To* DOG) Francis,
come here and be introduced!
(*The* DOG *leaves the bar and comes over to them. It is obviously intoxicated. It makes the* JOURNALISTS *a profound
bow*)

1ST J. That's a pretty cute hound of yours. What'll you take
for him?

ALAN Oh, I couldn't possibly sell him, thank you. Why, I
wouldn't be parted from Francis for a thousand pounds.
You've no idea how clever he is. It's quite uncanny, sometimes. . . . Francis, show the gentlemen what you can do.
(*The* DOG *attempts to balance a chair on his nose, but is too
drunk to do so. Suddenly he rushes out of the saloon and is
seen leaning over the rail of the ship*)

2ND J. Your canine friend appears to be slightly overcome.

ALAN Poor Francis! He'll be better soon. I hope it'll be a lesson to him. . . . Do please go on with what you were telling me. It's so awfully interesting. Tell me about some other
countries.

2ND J. All countries are the same. Everywhere you go, it's
the same: Nothing but a racket!
(*The* 1ST JOURNALIST *goes to the piano and begins to play*)

2ND J. (*singing*) The General Public has no notion
                    Of what's behind the scenes.
                 They vote at times with some emotion
                    But don't know what it means.
                    Doctored information
                    Is all they have to judge things by;
                 The hidden situation
                    Develops secretly.

CHORUS If the Queen of Poland swears,
                    If the Pope kicks his cardinals down the
                       stairs,
                    If the Brazilian Consul
                    Misses his train at Crewe,
                    If the Irish Clergy
                    Loose their en*erg*y
                    And dons have too much to do:
                 The reason is just simply this:
                    They're in the racket, too.

1ST J. To grasp the morning dailies you must
   Read between the lines.
 The evening specials make just nonsense
   Unless you've shares in mines.
 National estrangements
 Are not what they seem to be;
   Underground arrangements
 Are the master-key.

CHORUS If Chanel gowns have a train this year,
   If Morris cars fit a self-changing gear,
 If Lord Peter Whimsey
   Misses an obvious clue,
 If Wallace Beery
 Should act a fairy
   And Chaplain the Wandering Jew;
 The reason is
 Just simply this:
   They're in the racket, too!

(*The* DOG *re-enters the saloon. He holds out his arms to*
ALAN. *They dance. The* BARMAN *juggles with the cocktail*
shaker)

2ND J. There's lots of little things that happen
   Almost every day
 That show the way the wind is blowing
   So keep awake, we say.
 We have got the lowdown
   On all European affairs;
 To History we'll go down
   As the men with the longest ears.

CHORUS If the postman is three minutes late,
   If the grocer's boy scratches your gate,
 If you get the wrong number,
   If Cook has burnt the stew,
 If all your rock-plants
 Come up as dock-plants
   And your tennis-court turns blue;
 The reason is just simply this:
   You're in the racket, too!

CURTAIN

Chorus

Ostnia and Westland;
Products of the peace which that old man provided,
Of the sobriquet of Tiger senilely vain.
Do not content yourself with their identification,
Saying: This is the southern country with the shape of Corn-
wall,
Or the Danube receives the effluence from this: Or that must
shiver in the Carpathian shadow.
Do not comfort yourself with the reflection: "How very un-
English"
If your follies are different, it is because you are richer;
Your clocks have completed fewer revolutions since the com-
placent years
When Corelli was the keeper of the Avon Swan
And the naughty life-forcer in the norfolk jacket
Was the rebels' only uncle.
Remember more clearly their suaver images:
The glamour of the cadet-schools, the footmen and the enor-
mous hats.
But already, like an air-bubble under a microscope-slide, the
film of poverty is expanding
And soon it will reach your treasure and your gentlemanly
behaviour.
Observe, therefore, and be more prepared than our hero.

Scene III

(*Ostnia. Before the Palace. A* POLICEMAN *on duty. Enter* ALAN,
the JOURNALISTS *and the* DOG)

1ST J.   The trams are stopped, the streets are still,
Black flags hang from each window-sill
And the whole city is in mourning.
The King can't have died?

2ND J.   We had no warning.

1ST J.   You ask the bobby on the corner there.

2ND J.   Officer, what's happening here?

POLICEMAN   Twelfth of the month, sir: Execution Day
There's been a revolt, I'm sorry to say.

2ND J.   Another?
But you had one when I was here before.

POLICEMAN   When was that, sir?

2ND J.   Only last May.

POLICEMAN   Since then, we've had four.
We have them every fortnight, now;
But they're generally over without much row.
We round them up and then the King
  (*Salutes*)
Himself arranges everything.
Go inside and see. Strangers are always in-
vited.
I know His Majesty will be delighted.

1ST J.   Boy, what a scoop!
I'm cock a whoop!
Have you got your pencil?
It's quite essential.
(*The* JOURNALISTS *go into the Palace, followed by* ALAN *and the* DOG)

CURTAIN

Scene IV

(*Ostnia. A room in the Palace.* KING, QUEEN, COURTIERS, PRIESTS. *An organ voluntary is just finishing. The* MASTER OF CEREMONIES *approaches the* KING)

M.C.   Everything is ready, your Majesty.

KING   You've had a dress rehearsal, I hope? We don't want any hitches this time.

M.C.   Yes, your Majesty. I took your part myself. With a dummy revolver, of course.

KING   And what about my little suggestion?

M.C.   We've cut the Dies Irae, your Majesty.

KING   Good. I'm so glad you agree with me. I heard several
complaints last time, that it was too gruesome. As you
know, I am particularly anxious not to hurt anybody's feelings. It's a beautiful piece, of course, but one can't expect
them to be quite educated up to it yet. One has to make
allowances. . . . Oh, and by the way, you might tell the
male alto to moderate his top notes a bit. Last time, he gave
the Queen a headache.

M.C.   I will, your Majesty.

KING   Excellent. Then I think we can begin. Bring in the
prisoners. (*To the* QUEEN) My dear, your crown is a little
crooked. Allow me.
(*Solemn music. The* PRISONERS, *with their wives and
mothers, are brought in. The* PRISONERS *are workmen,
dressed neatly in their Sunday clothes. The women, like the
ladies of the court, are dressed in black*)

CHOIR   Requiem aeternam dona et lux perpetua luceat eis.

KING (*rising to address the* PRISONERS)   Gentlemen. I do not
intend to keep you long; but I cannot let this opportunity
slip by without saying how much I and the Queen appreciate
and admire the spirit in which you have acted and how extremely sorry we both are that our little differences can
only be settled in this er . . . somewhat drastic fashion.
   Believe me, I sympathise with your aims from the bottom
of my heart. Are we not all socialists nowadays? But as men
of the world I am sure you will agree with me that order
has to be maintained. In spite of everything which has
happened, I do want us to keep this solemn moment free
from any thought of malice. If any of you have a complaint
to make about your treatment, I hope you will say so now
before it is too late. You haven't? I am very glad indeed to
hear it. Before going on to the next part of the ceremony,
let me conclude by wishing you Bon Voyage and every happiness in the next world.
(*Music. The* PRISONERS *are led out. A footman brings a gold
revolver on a cushion and presents it to the* KING, *who follows the* PRISONERS)

CANTOR   Kyrie eleison.

CHOIR   Mars eleison.

CANTOR   Kyrie eleison.

CANTOR   Homo natus de muliere, brevi vivens tempore, repletur multis miseriis. Qui quasi flos egreditur et conteritur et
fugit velut umbra, et nunquam in eodem statu permanet.

Media via in morte sumus: quem quaerimus adjutorem
nisi te, Domine, qui pro peccatis nostris juste irasceris?

Sancte Zeus, sancto fortis, sancte et misericors Salvator
amaris mortis aeternae poenis ne tradas nos. Mars omnipotens. Frater Jovis, qui tollis peccata mundi.

CHOIR   Miserere nobis.

CANTOR   Qui tollis peccata mundi.

CHOIR   Miserere nobis.

CANTOR   Qui tollis peccata mundi.

CHOIR   Suscipe deprecationem nostram.

CANTOR   Qui sedet ad dextram Jovis.

CHOIR   Miserere nobis.
(Shots are heard, off. The Last Post is sounded)

CHOIR   Proficiscere Anima Ostniana, de hoc mundo.
*(Re-enter the KING. A footman brings a silk handkerchief to
clean the revolver. Another footman brings a basin of water
and a towel. The KING washes his hands. The four corpses
are brought in on stretchers)*

CHOIR   Rex tremendae majestatis, qui salvandos salvas gratis
salva me fons pietatis.
(Trumpet)

M.C.   Her Majesty the Queen will now address the bereaved.

QUEEN *(to the wives and mothers of the PRISONERS)*   Ladies
(or may I call you Sisters?). On this day of national sorrow,
my woman's heart bleeds for you. I too am a mother. I too
have borne the pangs of childbirth and known the unutterable comfort of seeing a little curly head asleep on my
breast. I too am a wife and have lain in the strong arms of
the beloved. Remember, then, in your loss, that in all you
suffer, I suffer with you. And remember that Suffering is
Woman's fate and Woman's glory. By suffering we are ennobled; we rise to higher things. Be comforted, therefore,
and abide patiently, strong in the hope that you will meet
your loved ones again in another and better world where
there are no tears, no pains, no misunderstandings; where we
shall all walk hand in hand from everlasting to everlasting.

M.C.   The ladies of the Court will offer the bereaved some
light refreshment.
(*The* LADIES *take round champagne and cakes to the* PRIS-
ONERS' WOMEN)

A WOMAN (*with a sudden hysterical scream*)   Murderers!!
(*All the* WOMEN *are instantly and politely removed by footmen. The* COURTIERS *cough and look at the ceiling in pained
embarrassment*)

KING   Poor things! They don't really mean it, you know.

QUEEN   They lead such terrible lives!
(*All the* COURTIERS *sigh deeply. The* LADIES *of the court
begin to admire the corpses*)

1ST LADY   How lovely they look:
    Like pictures in a children's book!

2ND L.   Look at this one. He seems so calm,
    As if he were asleep with his head in his arm.
    He's the handsomest, don't you think, of the four?
    How I wish I'd met him before!
    I'll put some blood on my hanky, a weeny spot,
    So that he never shall be forgot.

3RD L.   Oh Duchess, isn't he just a duck!
    His fiancée certainly had the luck.
    He can't have been more than nineteen, I should say.
    He must have been full of Vitamin A.

2ND L.   Dear Lady Emily,
    What a clever simile!

4TH L.   What beautiful hair; as white as wool!
    And such strong hands. Why, they're not yet cool!
    Lend me a pair of scissors, dear.
    I want a lock as a souvenir.

M.C.   Three Englishmen crave an audience with your Majesty.

KING   Oh, certainly, certainly. I'll see them at once.
(*Trumpet*)

M.C.   Mr. Alan Norman and friends.
(*Enter* ALAN *and the two* JOURNALISTS. *They kiss the* KING'S
hand)

KING   How do you do? Delighted to see anyone from England. I have very happy memories of visits there before the
War. The singing in King's Chapel was marvellous, quite
marvellous. And Melba, ah, delicious! Talking of which, I

hope you liked our singing today? I'm always most grateful for any criticisms. . . . How's London? My dear London! Those evenings at the Crystal Palace! What a building! What fireworks! I hear Regent Street is quite unrecognizable now. Dear me, how time flies, hm, indeed, yes. . . . But I mustn't bore you with an old man's memories. What can I do for you?

ALAN   I'm looking for Sir Francis Crewe:
        Is his name, Sire, known to you?

KING   Sir Francis Crewe? Hm, let me think. He wasn't one of your ambassadors, by any chance? I'm so stupid about names. (*To the* MASTER OF CEREMONIES) Ask the Court if they know anything about an Englishman called Sir Francis Crewe.
(*Trumpet*)

M.C.   Is an Englishman, Sir Francis Crewe,
        Familiar to anyone of you?
(*Silence*)

KING   You see? I'm so sorry. . . . But I tell you what: You might try the Red Light District. It's always full of foreign visitors. (*To* M.C.) Is the Crown Prince in?

M.C.   No, your Majesty.

KING   What a pity. He'd have been delighted to show you around. He's always going down there. It worries the Queen dreadfully, but I tell her not to take it to heart so: Boys will be boys. . . . Have you got a plan of the city?

M.C.   Here's one, your Majesty.

KING   Thanks. (*Opening the plan, to* ALAN) Come round on this side, you'll see better. Here's the Palace and here's the Palace Underground Station, just opposite. You take the tube to the Triangle: It's a two angel fare, I think. Then you take a number four tram to the Butter Kiln. After that, I'm afraid you'll have to walk. Keep left at the Cemetery.

M.C.   Excuse me, your Majesty, but the trams aren't running and everything's shut because of the executions.

KING   Of course! How silly of me to forget! Ring up the Broadcasting Station at once and have the mourning called off.
(M.C. *bows and retires*)

KING Well, goodbye, and I hope you find your friend. I'm
sorry we couldn't do more for you. . . . By the by, are you
sure you didn't see anything in the least bit out of taste in
our ceremony? I always think the English have such good
taste in matters of ritual. You didn't? That's very encour-
aging. When you get back to England, remember me to Lord
Harborne, if he's still alive. One of the real old English
eccentrics. Used to breakfast at midnight on champagne and
raw beef. . . . Won't you have a drink before you go?

ALAN No thank you, your Majesty. You see, we haven't got
much time.

KING Well, goodbye. Goodbye. (*Aside to the* M.C. *crossly*)
What on earth is the band-master thinking of? Tell him to
play something suitable at once, in honour of our guests.
(*As* ALAN *and the* JOURNALISTS *retire backwards, bowing,
the band begins to play "Rule, Britannia"*)

CURTAIN

Chorus

You with shooting-sticks and cases for field-glasses, your limou-
sines parked in a circle: who visit the public games, ob-
serving in burberries the feats of the body:
You who stand before the west fronts of cathedrals: appraising
the curious carving:
The virgin creeping like a cat to the desert, the trumpeting
angels, the usurers boiling:
And you also who look for truth: alone in tower:
Follow our hero and his escort on his latest journey: From the
square surrounded by Georgian houses, taking the lurch-
ing tram eastward
South of the ship-cranes, of the Slythe canal: Stopping at
Fruby and Drulger Street,
Past boys ball-using: shrill in alleys.
Passing the cinemas blazing with bulbs: bowers of bliss
Where thousands are holding hands: they gape at the tropical
vegetation, at the Ionic pillars and the organ solo.
Look left: The moon shows locked sheds, wharves by water,
On your right is the Power House: its chimneys fume gently
above us like rifles recently fired.

Look through the grating at the vast machinery: at the dyna-
    mos and turbines
Grave, giving no sign of the hurricane of steam within their
    huge steel bottles,
At the Diesel engines like howdahed elephants: at the dials
    with their flickering pointers:
Power to the city: where loyalties are not those of the family.
And now, enter:
O human pity, gripped by the crying of a captured bird wincing
    at sight of surgeon's lance,
Shudder indeed: that life on its narrow littoral so lucky
Can match against eternity a time so cruel!
The street we enter with setts is paved: cracked and uneven as
    an Alpine glacier,
Garbage chucked in the gutters has collected in the hollows in
    loathsome pools,
Back to back houses on both sides stretch: a dead-straight line
    of dung-colored brick
Wretched and dirty as a run for chickens.
Full as a theatre is the foul thoroughfare: some sitting like
    sacks, some slackly standing,
Their faces grey in the glimmering gaslight: their eyeballs
    drugged like a dead rabbit's,
From a window a child is looking, by want so fretted his face
    has assumed the features of a tortoise:
A human forest: all by one infection cancelled.
Despair so far invading every tissue has destroyed in these the
    hidden seat of the desire and the intelligence.

A little further, and now: Enter the street of some of your
    dreams:
Here come the untidy jokers and the spruce who love military
    secrets
And those whose houses are dustless and full of Ming vases:
Those rebels who have freed nothing in the whole universe
    from the tyranny of the mothers, except a tiny sensitive
    area:
Those who are ashamed of their baldness or the size of their
    members,
Those suffering from self-deceptions necessary to life
And all who have compounded envy and hopelessness into
    desire
Perform here nightly their magical acts of identification
Among the Chinese lanterns and the champagne served in
    shoes.

You may kiss what you like; it has often been kissed before.
Use what words you wish; they will often be heard again.

Scene V

(Ostnia. A street in the Red Light District. Each café has a small lighted peep-hole, resembling a theatre box-office. Above each of the four peep-holes is a sign-board with the name: TIGER JACK'S. YAMA THE PIT. COSY CORNER. MOTHER HUBBARD'S. *The heads of the four proprietors are visible at the peep-holes)*

FOUR PROPRIETORS *(singing together)*
> To Red Lamp Street you are all invited;
> Here Plato's halves are at last united.
> Whatever you dream of alone in bed,
> Come to us and we will make it real instead.

TIGER JACK   Do you feel like a bit of fun?
> At Tiger Jack's you will find it done.
> We've girls of eighty and women of four;
> Let them teach you things you never knew before.

PROPRIETRESS OF YAMA THE PIT
> Or does the thought of a thorough whipping
> By ladies in boots set your pulses skipping.
> At Yama the Pit you must pay a call
> And soon you won't be able to sit down at all.

BOSS OF COSY CORNER
> But perhaps you're a woman-scorner?
> Then step inside at the Cosy Corner.
> We've boys of every shape and size:
> Come and gaze into their great big eyes.

MOTHER HUBBARD   If you've taken a fancy to snow,
> Mother Hubbard's the place to go.
> With Cokey Minnie and Dopey Jim
> You can hold a party till the stars are dim.

ALL TOGETHER   Ladies and gentlemen, bear in mind
> Kisses in the graveyard are hard to find.
> "Tempus fugit," the poet said:
> So come to us at once for you will soon be dead.

(*Enter* ALAN, *the* JOURNALISTS *and the* DOG. *They are immediately accosted by two touts. The* 1ST TOUT *is very old and bleary. The* 2ND TOUT *is a boy of eight*)

1ST T.   Buy a post-card, guvnor?

2ND T.   Come wiv me. Good Jig-a-Jig.

ALAN   (*going up to* TIGER JACK)
          Good evening. Is Sir Francis Crewe,
          English, known perhaps to you?

TIGER JACK   Money, money
          Makes our speech as sweet as honey.
     (ALAN *gives money*)
          Now ask again
          And not in vain.

ALAN   Good evening. Is Sir Francis Crewe,
          English, known perhaps to you?

TIGER JACK   Phyllis, Lou,
          All of you,
          Have you heard of Sir Francis Crewe?

VOICES (*from within*)   A Francis I knew
          (a nice boy, too)
          And I a Crewe.
          But none of us know Sir Francis Crewe.

TIGER JACK   But stay.
          Here it is gay.

ALAN   No thank you, no.
          I must go.
     (*Moves on*)

1ST TOUT   Buy a post-card, guvnor?

2ND T.   Come wiv me. Good Jig-a-Jig.

ALAN   (*to* PROPRIETRESS OF YAMA THE PIT)
          Good evening. Is Sir Francis Crewe,
          English, known perhaps to you?

PROPRIETRESS OF Y. P.   Money, money
          Makes our speech as sweet as honey.
     (ALAN *gives money*)
          You must pay more.
     (ALAN *gives more*)
          Now speak again,
          Not in vain.

ALAN   Good evening. Is Sir Francis Crewe,
        English, known perhaps to you?

PROPRIETRESS OF Y. P.   Sue, Sue,
        That will do!
        He's already black and blue.
        Have you heard of Sir Francis Crewe?

SUE'S VOICE   I had an Englishman last year
        Who wore a pendant in each ear,
        Then there was one with a false nose:
        It wasn't either of them, I suppose?
        But stay,
        Here it is gay.

ALAN   No thank you, no.
        I must go.
    (*Moves away*)

1ST TOUT   Buy a post-card, guvnor?
    (2ND J. *buys one*)

1ST J. (*looking at it over his shoulder, in disgust*)
        Horrible hips and too much flesh:
        Why can't they get hold of someone fresh?

2ND T.   Come wiv me. Good Jig-a-Jig.

ALAN (*giving money to the* BOSS OF COSY CORNER)
        Good evening. Is Sir Francis Crewe,
        English, known perhaps to you?

BOSS OF C.C.
        You speak English? But I too!
        Am I acquaint with Sir Francis Crewe?
        Every English Lord come here.
        Is it he in the corner there?
        Wait a moment while I send
        For Willy. . . . Willy,
        How calls himself your English friend?

WILLY'S VOICE
        Harold. . . . Have you a cigarette for me?

BOSS OF C.C.   Is it he?
        Well, come inside and wait and see.
        Many come in after ten.
        Perhaps he will be one of them.

ALAN   No thank you, no.
        I must go.
    (*Moves away*)

1ST J.   Remember the sign.

2ND T.   Come wiv me. Good Jig-a-Jig.

(1ST J. *chases him away*)

2ND T.   And say the line.
(ALAN *knocks three times at the door of* MOTHER HUB-BARD'S)

MOTHER HUBBARD   The cupboard was bare.

ALAN   And yet the poor dog got some.
(*Gives money*)
Is the name Sir Francis Crewe,
English, known perhaps to you?

MOTHER HUBBARD
Wait a moment, please. I'll get Dopey Jim.
(*She disappears*)

1ST JOURNALIST   Hurry, hurry, do!
Our train leaves for Westland at twenty to.

2ND J.   Chuck up hunting for your boy friend.
It's clear that he's come to a sticky end.
(*The face of a drug addict, hopelessly dazed, appears at the peep-hole*)

ALAN   Good evening. Are you Mr. Dopey Jim?

ADDICT   That's what they call me here: Up there, in the world, I had another name. For I could dance lightly and spring high like a rubber ball in the air: being champion at Flash Green of all such sports.

ALAN   You know Flash Green? Why, that's where Sorbo Lamb came from! He went away seven years ago to look for Sir Francis Crewe. Did you ever meet him?

ADDICT   My mother bore no twins.

ALAN   Sorbo!

ADDICT   Alas.

ALAN   Oh, I am so glad! Whatever are you doing here? Have you seen Francis? Come along, we'll look for him together.

ADDICT   I may not leave this place.

ALAN   Do you mean they won't let you out? We'll soon see about that! There's four of us, and my dog can fight like a tiger. Just let them try to stop you!

ADDICT   You do not understand. (*Holds up his hands, which are free*) Don't you see these chains? My punishment and my reward. The light of your world would dazzle me and its noises offend my ears. Fools! How could you possibly appreciate my exquisite pleasures? Sometimes I lie quite still for days together, contemplating the flame of a candle or the oscillating shadow of a lamp. What revelations, what bottomless despairs! Please leave me alone.

ALAN   Sorbo. . . . Isn't there anything I can do?

ADDICT   Yes. Tell them at Flash Green that I am dead. More I ask not. Farewell.
(*He disappears*)

ALAN   What shall I do? What shall I do?
         I cannot find Sir Francis Crewe!

2ND J.   Pull your socks up, kid, and don't make a fuss!
         Come along to Westland now with us.
         Your friend may be there: You never know:
         And we'll show you all there is to show.
(*All three exeunt with* DOG, *singing*)
         If yer wants to see me agyne
             Then come to the stytion before the tryne.
         In the general wytin' 'all
             We'll see each other fer the very las' time of all!
(*The* FOUR PROPRIETORS *sing, accompanied by* FIRST TOUT *on the concertina and* SECOND TOUT *on the penny whistle*)

ALL TOGETHER
         Let us remember in a little song
         Those who were with us but not for long.
         Some were beautiful and some were gay
         But Death's Black Maria took them all away.

TIGER JACK
         Lucky Lil got a rope of pearls,
         Olive had autographed letters from earls,
         Grace looked lovely when she danced the Fern
         But Death took them yachting and they won't return.

YAMA THE PIT
         Prixie had a baron as a customer,
         He bought a zeppelin, just for her.
         You should have seen her with a hunting crop,
         But in Death's sound-proof room she's got to stop.

COSY CORNER
         Tony the Kid looked a god in shorts,

Phil was asked to Switzerland for winter sports,
Jimmy sent them crazy in his thick white socks,
But Death has shut them all up in a long black box.

MOTHER HUBBARD

Sammy and Di beat the gong round,
Wherever they walked there was snow on the ground.
Jessie and Colin had rings round their eyes
But Death put them where they can't get supplies.

ALL TOGETHER

When we are dead we shan't thank for flowers,
We shan't hear the parson preaching for hours,
We shan't be sorry to be white bare bone
At last we shan't be hungry and can sleep alone.

CURTAIN

Act Two

Scene I

(*Westland. A room in a lunatic asylum. At the back of the stage is a large portrait of a man in uniform: beneath which is written "Our Leader." The man has a loud-speaker instead of a face. The room is full of lunatics, male and female, who sit on their beds absorbed in various occupations or wander up and down the stage. On meeting each other, they exchange the Westland Salute: bringing the palm of the right hand smartly against the nape of the neck. Their manner is furtive and scared*)

1ST MAD LADY (*wanders across the stage, singing*)
> Seen when night was silent,
> The bean-shaped island
> And our ugly comic servant
> Who is observant
> O the verandah and the fruit
> The tiny steamer in the bay
> Startling summer with its hoot.
> You have gone away.

1ST LUNATIC (*whispering with* 2ND LUNATIC *in a corner*) Heard any rumours?

2ND L. Heaps!

1ST L. Oh, do tell me!

2ND L. Ssh! not so loud. I think they may be watching us.

1ST L. I tell you what: I've got a plan. We'll say goodbye now and then meet later, as if by accident.

2ND L. All right. But do be careful.
(*They exchange the Westland Salute and separate to their respective beds*)

(*Enter* TWO MEDICAL OFFICERS *with* ALAN *in a strait-waist-coat, in a wheeled chair*)

1ST M.O.   The Ostnia Frontier, wasn't it? They've sent us several beauties.

2ND M.O.   Yes.

1ST M.O.   What do they say?

2ND M.O.   Travelling with a dog.

1ST M.O.   Hm. Canophilia.

1ST M.O.   States he is looking for someone he doesn't know.

2ND M.O.   Phantasy Building. Go on.

1ST M.O.   Doesn't know the Westland Song.

2ND M.O.   Amnesia. Pretty serious. (*To* ALAN) Now you. Have you ever been to the North Pole?

ALAN   No.

1ST M.O.   Can you speak Chinese?

ALAN   No!

2ND M.O.   Do you dye your hair?

ALAN   No!

1ST M.O.   Was your mother a negress?

ALAN   No!!

2ND M.O.   Do you drink your bathwater?

ALAN   No!!!

1ST M.O.   Do you like my face?

ALAN (*losing his temper and yelling*)   No!!!!

1ST M.O.   Just as I feared, a typical case of negativism.

ALAN   What are you going to do? Let me out of here.

2ND M.O.   The gag, I think, don't you?

1ST M.O.   Yes, I think so.
(*They gag* ALAN)

2ND M.O.   Quite classic. He'll be an ornament to our collection.
(*Exeunt* MEDICAL OFFICERS)

2ND MAD LADY (*promenading with* 3RD M.L.)   The Leader says that next year he's going to put all us women into coops, like hens. And if we don't lay properly we shall be fattened for the Christmas Market.

3RD M.L.   Oh, what a lovely idea!

2ND M.L.   Yes, isn't it? And so beautiful, too. I mean, it will really make Motherhood sacred. And do away with all this horrible unwomanly nonsense about girls being independent. I'm sure *I* never wanted to be independent!

3RD M.L.   I should think not, indeed! (*Shivers*) Ugh, the idea!
(*Several* LUNATICS *surround a* LUNATIC *who is naked except for a bath-towel round his waist and has covered his body with smears of ink*)

NAKED LUNATIC   I am the President of the newly-formed League of the Forefathers of Westland, which the Leader himself has officially approved. After careful historical investigations, I have discovered that this is the exact costume worn by the inhabitants of Westland two thousand years ago. All modern dress is effeminate and foreign. The L.F.W. will lead Westland back to the manly customs of our ancestors. Down with Machinery! Down with knives and forks! Down with bath-rooms and books! Let us take to the woods and live on roots!
(*The other* LUNATICS, *in great excitement, begin tearing off their clothes and scratching on the floor, as if to dig up plants from the ground. Meanwhile, the* 1ST *and* 2ND LUNATICS *leave their beds and greet each other with much ceremony*)

1ST L.   Ah, good morning, my dear Baron!

2ND L.   Your Worship, this is indeed a pleasure!

1ST L.   Remarkably mild weather, is it not?

2ND L.   (*in the same tone of voice, nodding his head slightly in the direction of one of the other* LUNATICS)   I hear the Admiral is going to be denounced.

1ST L.   (*obviously delighted*)   Oh, I'm so sorry! Poor fellow! What for?

2ND L.   The usual. Byzantinism, of course: and Disaffection and Hoarding.

1ST L.   Tut, tut! I should never have believed it of him!

2ND L.   Oh, he's got a bad record. They say there's more than two thousand anonymous letters been written complaining about him to the Secret Police. *And all in invisible ink!*

1ST L.   Whew, that's nasty! (*Gleefully*) What do you think they'll do with him?

2ND L.   Send him to the Lead Mines, I expect.

1ST L. (*rubbing his hands together*)   Poor fellow!
(LUNATIC, *who has just fastened a flag to the end of his bed, shouts across to the* LUNATIC *sitting on the bed opposite*)

FLAG-LUNATIC   Hi, you! Why haven't you got your flag out? Don't you know what today is?

LUNATIC WITHOUT FLAG   Of course I do! It's the Day of National Rejoicing.

FLAG-L.   Then why don't you hang out your flag? If your flag isn't out, you can't be rejoicing.

L. WITHOUT F.   Of course I'm rejoicing. I was just sitting rejoicing quietly by myself when you disturbed me.

FLAG-L.   I don't believe you're rejoicing a bit! You don't look as if you were rejoicing.

L. WITHOUT F.   Well, neither do you, for that matter.

FLAG-L.   It doesn't matter how I look. I've got my flag out. Everyone knows *I'm* rejoicing.

L. WITHOUT F.   What are you rejoicing about?

FLAG-L.   I shan't tell you. What are you?

L. WITHOUT F.   I shan't tell you either.

FLAG-L.   Oh yes you will!

L. WITHOUT F.   No I won't!

FLAG-L.   Will!

L. WITHOUT F.   Won't!
(*The two* LUNATICS *adopt threatening attitudes and make horrible faces at each other*)
(*A trumpet*)

1ST LUNATIC   Silence everybody! The Leader is going to speak to us!
(*All the* LUNATICS *stand up and give the Westland Salute*)

THE VOICE OF THE LEADER (*through the loud-speaker in the picture*)   A short time ago, I was spending a week-end at a little village in the mountains. I sat on the verandah of the simple old Westland inn, looking out across the street to the meadows and the mountains beyond, those snow-capped peaks already flushed with the sunset glow. Westland swallows swooped in and out of the eaves overhead. In a doorway opposite, a young mother looked down at her suckling babe with ineffable Westland tenderness. In another, a Westland granny gazed out into the dusk with perfect serenity on her beautiful old face. Sturdy rosy-cheeked Westland youngsters romped in the new-mown hay a little further off. And presently down the street came the returning cattle, all their bells a-chiming in a sweet symphony, followed by the peasants, so honest, so thrifty, so frugal, wedded to the dear Westland earth in an eternal, holy marriage.

(*The* LUNATICS *have been much affected by this part of the speech. They sigh, shed tears and embrace each other with loud smacking kisses. One of the male lunatics takes flowers from a vase and distributes them among the ladies, who put the flowers in their hair*)

VOICE OF THE LEADER (*continuing*)   My eyes filled with tears. I could not speak just then. Perish the man, I thought, who can imagine this people capable of any base or unworthy deed! Westland! *Our* Westland! *My* Westland! All, all mine!

BUT:

A chill struck my heart. There *was* a shadow!

Not two hundred miles from where I stand, there is a Nation: trained to arms from infancy, schooled in military obedience and precision, saluting even in the cradle, splendidly equipped with every invention of modern science, able, resolute, taught to regard the individual as nothing and the State as all, scorning treaties as mere scraps of paper to be rent asunder when the interests of the State demand. My mind's eye saw the long silent grey ranks. I heard the shouting of the captains, the brazen call of the trumpet and the pawing of the chargers. And a voice said: Woe, woe to the unprepared: For their inheritance shall be taken away and their home be left desolate! (*The* LUNATICS *are now violently agitated. Some of them moan and shiver with fear, lie flat on the floor or crawl under the beds. Others blow trumpets, wave toy swords and strike down imaginary enemies*) From how slight a cause may proceed terrifying results! A piece of paper left by a picnic party which has inadvertently strayed over the frontier, a rash word in a letter about the superiority of Westland beer or a humorous sketch in a revue misunderstood: and in a moment it is too late. Destruction might come upon us like a thief in the night: while you are innocently dozing in your chair, or making an omelette or washing dishes at the kitchen sink. A secret cabinet meeting, a word whispered into the telephone and within half an hour, within twenty minutes, the black hordes of death are darkening the Westland air with their horrible shadows.

Picture the scene, Oh mothers! Your baby's face, pinched and puckered: Not by hunger, no. Sated with poison from the air it breathes, its tender little mouth agape, choking up froth and green bile.

Sons, see your aged father who has taught you to reverence truth and purity: see him caught as the house collapses, his skull smashed like an egg before your eyes by a falling beam!

Think, teachers, of the bombs falling suddenly in the playing-field! There goes that splendid young forward . . . ah! he's down: collapsing even as he reaches the goal-post, his beautiful hinged limbs contracted in agony!

(*Most of the* LUNATICS *are now staring up at the ceiling in fascinated horror, as though awaiting the aeroplanes' arrival*)

VOICE OF THE LEADER (*continuing*) Nor is this all. The flame once lit would spread into a universal conflagration. England, Iceland, Ecuador and Siam would flare and within a week our civilisation, all that our statesmen and thinkers, our poets and musicians, have travailed for down the ages of history, would lie a smoking ruin!

No, this must not be! Westland is the guardian of Europe. We love peace (I say it in absolute confidence) more than any other country. Let us be ready and able to enforce it. We must build an air force of such a magnitude that any enemy, however ferocious, will think twice before daring to strike. Within three weeks we must have a million planes, not one less! We must make a stupendous effort. No sacrifice is too great. I expect every man, woman and child in Westland to help. Give up that cigar after lunch, do without an extra lipstick, abstain from your favourite sweets. Is that too much to ask when the safety of the Homeland is at stake? Our responsibilities are vast: Let us be worthy of them. And God help us all.

(*Tremendous enthusiasm. The* LUNATICS *jump up and down in their delight, cheer, embrace, pillow-fight, and box each other's ears*)

THE LUNATIC WITH THE FLAG Let's build a great big plane for our Leader!

LUNATICS   Oh yes! Let's!!

(*The* LUNATICS *begin dragging beds together and piling furniture upon them. The din is tremendous. Suddenly, at the window, appear the heads of the* TWO JOURNALISTS *and the* DOG. *They peer cautiously into the room, looking for* ALAN. *After a moment, they hastily withdraw*)

1ST LUNATIC (*who evidently considers himself the most important of them all and is rather piqued that the plane-building should have been suggested by someone else, stands on a chair and begins clapping his hands to command attention; after some time, he succeeds in getting the* LUNATICS *to stop working and listen to him*)   Madmen of Westland!

In this hour of supreme crisis, I feel called upon to say a few words. This is my message to you all. Let us never forget that we are Westlanders first and madmen second. As Westlanders, we have a great tradition to uphold. Westland has always produced ten per cent. more lunatics than any other country in Europe. And are we going to show ourselves inferior to our forefathers? Never!

(*The* JOURNALISTS *reappear at the window, try the strength of the bars and shake their heads. The* DOG *is seen arguing with them in dumb show and indicating that they come with him. They all disappear*)

1ST LUNATIC (*continuing*)   Of recent years, there have appeared in our midst, masquerading as men of science, certain Jews, obscurantists and Marxist traitors. These men have published enormous books, attempting to provide new classifications and forms of lunacy. But we are not deceived. No foreign brand of madness, however spectacular, however noisy or pleasant, will ever seduce us from the grand old Westland Mania. What was good enough for our forefathers, we declare, is good enough for us! We shall continue to go mad in the time-honoured Westland way.

A LUNATIC   Three cheers for the Westland Loonies!

ALL   Hurrah! Hurrah! Hurrah!

ANOTHER LUNATIC (*suddenly seeing* ALAN)   Hullo, you! Why don't you cheer?

(*All the* LUNATICS *stop shouting and look at* ALAN. *At this moment, unseen by any of them, the* TWO JOURNALISTS *enter the room by a door on the right of the stage*)

ANOTHER LUNATIC   His mouth's tied up! He's got the tooth-ache!

(*Begins to giggle*)

ANOTHER LUNATIC   He's been sent here to spy on us!

ANOTHER   He's been hoarding butter!

ANOTHER   He's insulted the Leader!

ANOTHER   Rumour-monger!

ANOTHER   Non-Aryan!

ANOTHER   Separatist!

ANOTHER   Grumbler!
(*All this time, they draw closer to him, rushing forward in turns to tug at his hair, tweak his nose or pull his ears*)

A LUNATIC   Squirt water at him!

ANOTHER   Put a rat in his bed!

ANOTHER   Tickle his toes!

ANOTHER   Shave off his eyebrows!

ANOTHER   I say, chaps! Let's do something really exciting! Let's put lavatory paper under his chair and burn it!
(*They seem about to make a final rush at* ALAN, *when the* JOURNALIST *speaks, in a very loud and impressive voice, like a conjurer*)

1ST J.   Ladies and Gentlemen! (*All the* LUNATICS *turn round to stare at him*) I am about to show you a simple but extremely interesting scientific experiment. (*Holds up his hand*) Now, watch the duck's head and please keep absolutely still while I count a hundred. One. Two. Three. . . .
(*While the* 1ST JOURNALIST *is counting, the* 2ND JOURNALIST, *on all fours, worms his way through the crowd to* ALAN'S *side and begins hastily undoing the ropes and straps*)

2ND J. (*in a low voice, to* ALAN)   Gosh, that was a close shave!

ALAN   How on earth did you find me?

2ND J.   Your dog guided us here. That animal is better than the whole of Scotland Yard put together. He's outside now, keeping guard over the warders until we get you loose. . . . Curse these knots!
(*Meanwhile, the* 1ST J. *continues to count. But the* LUNATICS *are becoming less attentive. Those who are standing close to* ALAN *begin to take an interest in the* 2ND JOURNALIST'S *activities*)

LUNATIC   What are you doing that for?

2ND J.   Can't you see? I'm tying him up tighter. The ropes had got loose. See this one? (*He holds it up*) It had slipped right off. (*He throws it away*) No good at all.
(*He continues to unfasten the other ropes and straps*)

LUNATIC   I'll help you.
(*Begins to refasten the straps*)

2ND J.   Don't bother, old boy. I can manage by myself.
(*Unfastens them again*)

LUNATIC   It's no bother. I like helping people. I'm a Boy Scout.

2ND J.   Well, do your day's good deed by leaving me alone, see?

LUNATIC   I don't think that would be a good deed, would it?

2ND J.   You bet it would!

LUNATIC   Perhaps you're right. But I'd better just ask the others what they think. (*In a very loud voice*) I say!
(*All the* LUNATICS *turn round to look at him*)

2ND J.   Holy Moses, that's torn it!

1ST LUNATIC   What are you doing with our prisoner?

2ND L.   Where's your warrant?

3RD L.   Habeas Corpus!

4TH L.   It's a rescue!

5TH L.   Stand by the doors!

OTHERS   Fire! Murder! Treason!
(*The* 1ST JOURNALIST, *now disregarded, rushes to the Leader's picture and gets behind it*)

1ST J. (*through the loud-speaker*)   Company! Fall in!
(*The* LUNATICS *immediately form a double rank, facing the Leader's picture.* 2ND J. *continues feverishly with the work of untying* ALAN)

1ST J.   Slooope Hyppp!
(*The* LUNATICS *go through the motion of sloping arms*)

1ST J.   Oddah Hyppp!
(LUNATICS *order arms*)

1ST J.   Slooope Hyppp! (*They do so*) Oddah Hyppp! (*They do so*)

2ND J. (*to* ALAN)   That's all the drill he knows! (*Undoing*

the last strap) There! Come on, this is where we scoot!
(*They rush out*)

1ST J.   Company! Man the aeroplane! Fall out!
(*The* LUNATICS *rush to the structure of beds and scramble upon it. The* 1ST JOURNALIST *slips from behind the picture and runs out after the others*)

1ST LUNATIC   Start her up!
(*The* LUNATICS *imitate the roaring of the engines*)

1ST L.   Off we go! Faster! Faster! She's left the ground! We're rising! Higher! Higher!
(*The* LUNATICS *wave their handkerchiefs and grimace at the audience*)

A MAD LADY   Isn't the view gorgeous?

2ND MAD LADY   Look, there's the asylum. Just a tiny little speck!

A MAD LADY   I'll spit down the chimney!
(*Spits*)

THE PILOT   Hold on tight! I'm going to loop the loop!
(*Shrieks of dismay. The* LUNATICS *heave the beds up on end until the whole structure collapses. General confusion.* ALAN, *the* JOURNALISTS *and the* DOG *peep in for a moment at the window and disappear laughing*)

CURTAIN

Chorus

Paddington. King's Cross. Euston. Liverpool Street:
Each hiding behind a gothic hotel its gigantic greenhouse
And the long trains groomed before dawn departing at ten,
Picking their way through slums between the washing and the
          privies
To a clear run through open country,
Ignoring alike the cathedral towns in their wide feminine val-
          leys, and the lonely junctions.
In such a train sit Norman and his dog
Moving backwards through Westland at a mile a minute
And playing hearts with their two friends on an open mackin-
          tosh:

Picture the Pullman car with its deft attendants
And the usual passengers: the spoilt child, the corridor addict,
The lady who expects you to admire her ankles: the ostenta-
    tious peruser of important papers, etc. etc.
They have been travelling all day, it is late afternoon.
Outside the windows of the warm sealed tube, as a background
    to their conversation,
Imagine a hedgeless country, the source of streams;
Such as the driver, changing up at last, sees stretching from
    Hartside east and south,
Deadstones above Redan, Thackmoss, Halfpenny Scar,
Two Top and Muska, Pity Mea, Bullpot Brow:
Land of the ring ousel: a bird stone-haunting, an unquiet bird.

Scene II

(*In a railway-train.* ALAN, *the* TWO JOURNALISTS *and the* DOG
are playing cards. A little distance off sits the FINANCIER, *at
present half hidden by his newspaper*)

1ST J.   Your lead, Alan.
    (*Alan plays.* 1ST J. *plays a card*)

ALAN (*to* 2ND J.)   Eight to beat.

2ND J. (*looking at* DOG)   Hm . . . shall I risk it? No, I don't
think so.
    (*He plays a card. The* DOG *also plays a card*)

1ST J. (*suspiciously*)   Hullo, you short-suited? Here, let's see
your hand.
    (*He reaches out to take the* DOG's *cards. The* DOG *growls and
    refuses to show them*)

ALAN   Show them to me, Francis. Good Dog! (DOG *reluctantly
    hands over the cards*) But you've got Slippery Anne here,
    look!

2ND J.   Darned if he hasn't been cheating again.

ALAN (*indignantly*)   He wasn't cheating! He just doesn't understand the rules, do you Doggy?

1ST J.   If you ask me, that Dog of yours understands a damn
    sight too much. He's too smart by half. (*Yawns*) Well,
    gentlemen, you've cleaned me out. I'll go and stretch myself

a bit. (*Standing up, he catches sight of the* FINANCIER: *sits down abruptly: to* 2ND J., *in a whisper*) Great God, man, look!

2ND J.   Where?

1ST J.   There!

2ND J.   Snakes! It isn't . . . ?

1ST J.   Bet you a fiver it is!

2ND J.   The papers say he's in Manchukuo.

1ST J.   Just eyewash!

2ND J.   Boy! I believe you're right!

ALAN (*loudly*)   What's all the fuss about!

1ST J.   Ssh!

2ND J.   Sssh!!

ALAN   You might tell a fellow!

1ST J. (*stage whisper*)   Grabstein! Sitting just behind you!

ALAN   Grabstein?

2ND J.   Ssh!

ALAN   Who's he when he's at home?

1ST J.   Oh boy, where were you educated? (*Wearily, to* 2ND J.) Go on, you tell him.

2ND J.   President of the X.Y.Z.

1ST J.   Chairman of the Pan-Asiatic.

2ND J.   Practically owns South America.

1ST J.   The biggest crook in Europe. Got his finger in everything. Whatever happens, he's in on the ground floor. Why, he even gets to hear of things before *we* do, sometimes!

ALAN   I say! Not really! I wonder if he knows where Francis is?

2ND J.   Most likely he does. The question is: would he tell you?

1ST J. (*winking at* 2ND J.)   Go and ask him.

ALAN   Shall I really?

2ND J. (*winking at* 1ST J.)   Atta boy!

ALAN (*doubtfully*)   All right. . . . If you don't think he'd mind?

1ST J.   Hell! Why should he?

2ND J.   He'll welcome you with open arms.

1ST J.   (*artfully*)   By the way, you might ask him a few other
questions while you're about it. Find out what holdings he
has in Sahara Electrics.

2ND J.   And how much it cost him to start the war in Spits-
bergen?

1ST J.   And what became of the Cloaguan Prime Minister
after the Platinum Scandals?

ALAN   I say, hold on a minute: I shall never remember all
that! Just give me time to write it down.
(*He takes a piece of paper from his pocket and makes notes.
The* JOURNALISTS *whisper instructions into his ear*)

ALAN   But won't he think me awfully inquisitive?

2ND J.   Oh, he loves being asked questions. . . . Just go up
to him and say: "Potts." That's the name of a very dear
friend of his. It'll put him in a good temper at once.

ALAN   (*doubtfully*)   Righto.
(*He approaches the* FINANCIER. *The* JOURNALISTS *shake
hands with each other in ecstasies of delight*)

1ST J.   Oh boy, I wouldn't have missed this for a thousand
pounds!
(*During the following scene, the* JOURNALISTS *take photographs and make notes*)

ALAN   (*rather nervously*)   Potts.
(*The* FINANCIER *looks up from his newspaper, stares at him
for a moment, turns deadly pale. Then, with a shrug of his
shoulders, he takes a cheque-book from his pocket and un-
screws the cap of his fountain-pen*)

FINANCIER   (*with a deep sigh*)   How much do you want?

ALAN   I beg your pardon, sir. I don't quite understand.

FINANCIER   (*more firmly*)   I'll give you a thousand: Not one
penny more. And you understand that I'm doing it because
I don't choose to be annoyed at this particular moment. I
have reasons for remaining incognito. I suppose you counted
on that? Very well . . . But let me warn you, if you're fool
enough to imagine that you can play this game twice, you
were never more mistaken. I have ways of dealing with
gentry of your sort. Understand?

ALAN I'm awfully sorry, sir. But I think you must be making some mistake. . . . I only wanted to ask you a few questions. . . . It's frightful cheek of me, I know. . . .

FINANCIER Oh, a journalist, eh? That's bad enough. Still, as you're here, I suppose I can let you have five minutes. Ask away. . . .

ALAN (*consulting his notes*) First of all, did you forge the report on the diamond mines on Tuesday Island?
(*The* FINANCIER *gasps*)

ALAN (*continuing hurriedly*) Secondly, is it true that you staged the fake attempt on the Prince of Hellespont in order to corner the rubber market?

FINANCIER Do you seriously expect me to answer that?

ALAN Well, no sir. To be quite candid, I don't. Please don't be angry. . . . Thirdly, did you have the men murdered who were going to show up the Bishop of Pluvium?

FINANCIER (*laughs*) Young man, you amuse me. Very well, since you're the first newspaper man who's ever dared to talk to me like this, I'll tell you the truth. The answer to all your three questions is: "Yes. I did." There! Now you've got a grand story, haven't you? Go and ask your editor to print it and he'll kick you out into the street. What's your paper, by the way? Ten to one, I own it.

ALAN The Pressan Ambo Parish Magazine.

FINANCIER Never heard of it. But I'll buy it tomorrow, lock, stock and barrel. How much would your boss take, do you suppose?

ALAN I'm afraid I couldn't tell you that, sir. You see I only write for it occasionally. A bit of poetry now and then. Awful rot, I expect you'd think it.

FINANCIER (*groans*) Good God! Don't say you're a poet too!

ALAN Oh rather not, sir!

FINANCIER Glad to hear it. Of course, mind you, I've nothing against poets, provided they make good. They say that one or two fellows at the top of the tree are earning as much as four thousand a year. I doubt it myself. . . . But the fact remains that most of them are moral degenerates or Bolsheviks, or both. The scum of the earth. My son's a poet.

ALAN   I'm sorry, sir.

FINANCIER (*sentimentally*)   It's been the greatest disappoint-
ment of my whole life. Who have I got to work for, to be
proud of? Nobody. And my wife encourages him; the bitch.
As long as she's got her cocaine and her gigolos, we can all
go to hell as far as she's concerned. . . . I don't know why
I'm telling you all this.

ALAN (*politely*)   It's rotten luck for you, sir.

FINANCIER   Look here. I've taken a fancy to you. Will you be
my secretary? Starting at five thousand a year, with all
extras. Yes or no?

ALAN   It's most awfully kind of you, sir: but I'm afraid I
can't. . . .

FINANCIER (*emotionally*)   There, you see! I knew it! You
don't like me. None of them like me. Wherever I go I see it.
I can't so much as get a really friendly smile out of a railway-
porter, though Heaven knows I tip them enough. . . .
    (*Sings. Accompaniment by dining-car attendant with gong*)
        When I was young I showed such application,
            I worked the whole day long;
        I hoped to rise above my station,
            To rise just like a song:
        I did so want to be a hero
            In just a rich man's way
        But I might just as well be Nero,
            And this is all I have to say:

CHORUS (*with* ATTENDANT *and* JOURNALISTS)
            Why are they so rude to me?
            It seems so crude to me,
            I want to be friendly
            But it's no good, for
            No one has love for me,
            Only a shove for me,
            They bait me and hate me, I'm
            Misunderstood.

FINANCIER
            I've founded hospitals and rest-homes,
                Subscribed to public funds,
            Promoted schemes for planning Best Homes
                And built a school for nuns.
            I've studied all the Italian Masters,
                I've tried to read French books,

> But all my efforts seem disasters:
>   I only get such nasty looks.

CHORUS
>   Why are they so rude to me, . . . etc.

FINANCIER   Now what is it? Tell me straight out; don't be afraid. Is it my face? Is it my voice? Is it my manner? Or are you all just jealous of my damned money?

ALAN   It isn't that, sir. Really it isn't. But you see . . . I'm not free. I've got a kind of job . . . if you can call it a job. . . .

FINANCIER   Chuck it. I'll give you six thousand.

ALAN   You see, sir, it's not that kind of job: that you can chuck up, I mean. . . . I've got to look for someone. He's Sir Francis Crewe, Bart. At least, he's Bart if he's alive. . . . That's what I really came to ask you about. . . . He ran away from home ten years ago. I thought you might happen to know where he is.

FINANCIER   What do you take me for? A nursemaid?
    (*The train stops. A* PORTER *looks in at the window*)

PORTER   All change for Malago, Reykjavik and Omsk!

FINANCIER   I must get out here. Will you take ten thousand? Yes or no? It's my last word.

ALAN   I'm truly most terribly sorry, but. . . .

FINANCIER   You're more of a fool than I took you for. (*Sentimentally*) Write to me sometimes and tell me how you're getting on. It would be so lovely to get a letter which had nothing to do with business!

ALAN   Rather, sir!

FINANCIER   Oh, by the way, a good place to look for that Baronet of yours would be Paradise Park. This train'll take you there. It's where most wasters and cranks land up sooner or later, if they've still got some cash to be swindled out of. You'll meet my dear son, among others. Perhaps you'll be able to knock some sense into him. Tell him I offer him a hundred thousand if he'll stop writing his drivel and clean a sewer. Goodbye.

ALAN   Goodbye, sir. Thanks awfully.
    (*The* FINANCIER, *with the help of* ALAN *and the* PORTER, *descends from the train*)

1ST J. (*to* 2ND J.)   Quick, we mustn't lose sight of him! If we follow him now, maybe we'll get the dope on that Dripping Merger, after all!
(*They leave the train*)

2ND J. (*to* ALAN)   You coming, Kid?

ALAN   I can't, I'm afraid. I've just got a new clue.

1ST J.   Well, good luck.

2ND J.   Ta ta.

ALAN   Goodbye, and thanks most awfully for all you've done.
(*The train moves on.* ALAN *waves from the window. Then he turns to the* DOG)

ALAN   Well, Doggy. We're all alone, now. Just you and me.
(*He puts his arm round the* DOG's *neck*) I wonder what Iris is doing? Oh dear, I wish we weren't such a long way from home. . . .
(*He gazes sadly out of the window*)

CURTAIN

Chorus

Happy the hare at morning, for she cannot read
The Hunter's waking thoughts. Lucky the leaf
Unable to predict the fall. Lucky indeed
The rampant suffering suffocating jelly
Burgeoning in pools, lapping the grits of the desert,
The elementary sensual cures,
The hibernations and the growth of hair assuage:
Or best of all the mineral stars disintegrating quietly into light.
But what shall men do, who can whistle tunes by heart,
Know to the bar when death shall cut him short, like the cry of
    the shearwater?
We will show you what he has done.
How comely are his places of refuge and the tabernacles of his
    peace,
The new books upon the morning table, the lawns and the
    afternoon terraces!
Here are the playing-fields where he may forget his ignorance
To operate within a gentleman's agreement: twenty-two sins
    have here a certain licence.

Here are the thickets where accosted lovers combatant
May warm each other with their wicked hands,
Here are the avenues for incantation and workshops for the
    cunning engravers.
The galleries are full of music, the pianist is storming the keys,
    the great cellist is crucified over his instrument,
That none may hear the ejaculations of the sentinels
Nor the sigh of the most numerous and the most poor; the thud
    of their falling bodies
Who with their lives have banished hence the serpent and the
    faceless insect.

Scene III

(*The gardens of Paradise Park. A beautifully-kept lawn. Numbers of people are walking about the stage in sports clothes of various kinds or propelling themselves hither and thither in invalid chairs. Some lie on the grass absorbed in books. In the background are two large trees. In one of the trees sits the* POET, *smoking cigarettes: In the other are two* LOVERS *dressed in nursery-teapot-Dutch costumes. In the distance, the band plays a waltz*)

CHORUS   When you're in trouble,
        When you get the air,
    When everything returns your ring
        Do not despair, because although
    Friends may forsake you
        And all skies are dark
    You can be gay if you just step this way
        Into Paradise Park.

    Was it a tiring day
        On your office stool?
    Has your wife all your life
        Made you feel a fool? Don't cry, for though
    Landlords perplex you
        And all bosses frown,
    In Paradise Park you can feel a young spark
        And do them down!
(*Enter* ALAN *and the* DOG. *They approach the* POET'S *tree*)

ALAN (*to* POET)   Excuse me, sir. Is this Paradise Park?

POET   ἔστιν θάλασσα, τίς δέ νιν κατασβέσαι.

ALAN   I beg your pardon?

POET   Nil nimium studeo, Caesar, tibi velle placere nec scire utrum sis albus aut ater homo.

ALAN   I'm awfully sorry, but I don't understand. Do you speak English?

POET   Nessum maggior dolore che ricordarsi del tempo felice.

ALAN   I know a little German, if that will do. . . . Entschuldigen Sie, bitte. Koennen Sie mir sagen, ob dies ist der Garten von Paradies?

POET   Dans l'an trentième de mon age. . . . (ALAN *begins to move off*) Oh well, if you insist on talking our filthy native language, I suppose I must. . . . Give me a cigarette. I've finished mine.

ALAN   I'm so sorry. . . . Of course. . . .
    Is the name Sir Francis Crewe
    Known by any chance to you?

POET   Did you like it?

ALAN   Er . . . ?

POET   I'm so glad you did! I wrote it!

ALAN   Wrote what?

POET   "Advances New," of course. Now tell me, which section did you like the best? *Mandrake* is the best technically, of course. But *Cinders* is more the real me, I think.

ALAN   I'm afraid you misunderstood me. I said Sir Francis Crewe. I've been looking for him.

POET   "Your chase had a beast in view."

ALAN   You know where he is?

POET   Well, of course.

ALAN   Where?

POET   (*tapping his forehead*)   Here. Everything's here. You're here. He's here. This park's here. This tree's here. If I shut my eyes they all disappear.

ALAN   And what happens if I shut *my* eyes? Do you disappear, too?

POET   (*crossly*)   No, of course not! I'm the only real person in the whole world.

ALAN   Well, suppose your tree was cut down? It wouldn't be there when you looked for it.

POET   Nonsense! The axe wouldn't exist unless I thought of it. The woodcutter wouldn't exist either.

ALAN   Isn't your Father the famous financier?

POET   I used to think so. But I got tired of that and forgot him. Give me another cigarette.

(*As he leans down, the* DOG *jumps up and bites his hand*)

POET   (*nursing his hand*)   Why can't you keep your blasted dog in order? Oh, my poor hand!

ALAN   I'm most dreadfully sorry. But you see, he's never seen a real person before. When you're only an imaginary dog and have been eating imaginary biscuits all your life, a real hand must taste simply delicious. You couldn't resist it, could you, Francis old boy? (*To* POET) Never mind. Just shut your eyes and you'll forget all about us.

POET   (*with his eyes shut*)   Oh, I've forgotten *you* long ago! It's my hand I keep remembering!

(ALAN *and* DOG *move on to the* LOVERS' *tree*)

1ST LOVER   Little white dove, it's you that I love,
            Fairer than hollyhocks far!
            How nice and how neat
            Are your dear little feet!
            You make my heart beat!
            How terribly sweet, how terribly sweet,
            How terribly sweet you are!

(*They hug each other, taking no notice of* ALAN)

ALAN   Excuse me, please, disturbing you:
            But have you heard of Sir Francis Crewe?

2ND L.   Have you, darling?

1ST L.   Oh, pretty starling!
            Say that again
            And again and again!
            I love to watch your cheek
            Move when you speak!

2ND L.   Oh dearest, you mustn't go on so!
            There's a nice man down below
            And there is something he wants to know.

1ST L.   Good morning. Let me introduce my wife.
            We're going to be lovers all our life:

> Two as one and one as two.
> Is there anything we can do?

ALAN   Have you heard of Sir Francis Crewe?

1ST L.   Sir Francis Crewe? Do *you* know, sweet?
> Was that the funny old man on the seat
> Who looked so cross when I gave you a kiss?

2ND L.   You were so naughty! Oh!

1ST L. (*embracing her*)   Just like this!

ALAN   No, he's not very old.

1ST L.   Darling, you're cold.
> Put my coat on. What dear little shoulders!
>   (ALAN *begins to move off*)
> Don't go, old man. You mustn't scold us.
> We'd ask you up, but there isn't room.
> But when we've a large tree you must come.
>   (ALAN *moves off*)

2ND L.   Wonderful boy, you're all my joy!

1ST L.   I'd like to eat you for tea!

2ND L.   You're so tender and strong!

1ST L.   You're just like a song!

2ND L.   To you I belong!

BOTH   You cannot do wrong, you cannot do wrong,
> You cannot do wrong with me!

(*Two* FEMALE INVALIDS *in bath-chairs move to the front of the stage*)

1ST INVALID   How many stitches have you got?

2ND I. (*proudly*)   Four.

1ST I.   Oh do let me see!

2ND I.   Not now, wait till the dressing.

1ST I.   Oh please! Just one peep!

2ND I.   Very well.
  (*Shows wound*)

1ST I.   Oh, what a beauty!

2ND I.   Don't tell Alice. Promise! She's terribly jealous. They only put two in her. When they told her after she'd come round, she cried.

1ST I.   Betty's a lucky girl. She's got tubes.

2ND I.   She hasn't!

1ST I.   Yes! Only it's a secret. She told me all about it at breakfast. My dear, they took out *everything!* She even thinks they may give her a real silver set!

2ND I.   How too marvellous! Won't her Ted be proud?

ALAN   (*approaching them*)   Excuse me.
Is the name Sir Francis Crewe
Known perhaps to either of you?

1ST I.   What's he got?

ALAN   Got?

1ST I.   What illness has he got?

ALAN   What? Is he ill?

1ST I.   Of course he is, silly: if he's here. Aren't you?

ALAN   No. I don't think so.

BOTH INVALIDS   (*turning their chairs away*)   How *disgusting!*
(*Enter a* COLONEL *in a bath-chair, with an ear-trumpet*)

ALAN   Excuse me, sir, but is Sir Francis Crewe
Known by any chance to you?

COLONEL   Can't hear a word, sir. Stone deaf, thank God!
(ALAN *wanders off asking various other people. The two* INVALIDS *return*)

1ST I.   Have you ever noticed his hands? Just like a violinist's.

2ND I.   I wonder who he'll choose for the operation today?

1ST I.   (*blushing*)   Well, I don't like to be presumptuous, but I think. . . .

2ND I.   No? Not really!

1ST I.   (*complacent*)   Hm, hm. . . .

2ND I.   My dear, I *do* congratulate you!

1ST I.   It was only a look, mind you: but you can't mistake him when he looks at you like that. Made me feel quite goosey! Oh look, there he is coming out of the ward! Quickly, dear, lend me your powder-puff. I must look my best when I go under. . . . Ooh, the brute! He's chosen that new case! It isn't fair!
(*Bursts into tears*)

2ND I.   There, there, darling! Don't take on so! It's sure to be you next time.

1ST I. (*blubbering*)   I don't care! I was counting on it to-day. It's too bad! He only came in this morning.
(*The* INVALIDS *move away as the* SURGEON *and* ANAESTHE-TIST *enter, followed by a* NURSE *pushing* CHIMP EAGLE, *the patient, on a wheeled stretcher*)

SUR.   What do you think, Doctor! Intraspinal or general?

AN.   Oh, general in this case.

SUR.   You're playing on Saturday, aren't you?

AN.   Yes, I hope so.

SUR.   Good man! We can't do without you in the deep. Young Waters is playing too. He's no snyde at the game.
(*Exeunt* SURGEON *and* ANAESTHETIST)

CHIMP EAGLE (*recognising* ALAN)   Hullo Alan!

ALAN   Why, it's Chimp Eagle! What's the matter with you, old man?

CHIMP   A strike down at the docks. The Police had a machine-gun. Got me in the guts. . . . I say, you aren't in with our lot, too, are you?

ALAN   No, I'm looking for Francis.

CHIMP   Francis: The missing heir! (*Smiles*) How long ago that seems. I'd forgotten all about him.

ALAN   Chimp . . . did you ever find out anything?

CHIMP   I can't remember. . . . No. . . . That is, yes. . . . I. . . .
(*He is too exhausted to say more*)

NURSE (*coming forward*)   Now then, sir: That's enough. You're tiring the patient.

ALAN (*withdrawing to the other side of stage, to* DOG)   Oh Doggy, what shall I do? They're coming to take him away. And I *must* speak to him again somehow. . . . Oh dear . . . !
(*The* DOG *gives* ALAN *a glance, as much as to say: Watch me! Then it runs across the stage and begins fawning on the* NURSE)

NURSE   What a lovely doggie! May I pat him? (*The* DOG *jumps at her and begins tearing off her uniform*) Oh! Oh! Help!

ALAN   What on earth are you doing? Naughty dog! Stop it this minute! (*Suddenly understanding*) No, don't stop. Splendid! Good dog! I'll help.

(They strip the NURSE *of her uniform and tie her up. The* DOG *is dressed by* ALAN *in the* NURSE'S *uniform. They dump the* NURSE *in a disused bath-chair and cover her with a rug. Scarcely are they ready when the* SURGEON *returns)*

SUR.   Nurse, what the Dickens are you waiting for? Bring the patient at once, please.

(The DOG *wheels* CHIMP EAGLE *out.* ALAN *follows at a discreet distance)*

CHORUS   There's consolations here to suit
        Every mood and means:
    Skating-rinks, booths for drinks,
        Gambling-machines and switchbacks and
    Art for the Highbrow
    And Sport for the Low-:
    Life is a lark at Paradise Park;
        For the fast and the slow.

CURTAIN

Chorus

Seeding and harvest, the mating of lions, the divergent migrations are themes for another occasion than this:
In this white world of order and professional attentions
Of airy wards, the smell of iodoform, the squeak of rubber-tyred stretchers
Solar time is unreal.
Against these walls the waves of action and charity must wash in vain.
1600 beds
10 theatres magnificently equipped
A special wing for infectious cases
A chapel, a mortuary, labs for research, and really adequate nursing accommodation
And, opened last year, a solarium for the convalescent.
1600 beds: in each one patient, apparently alone;
One who has forsaken family and friends; to set up house here with his hostile shadow.
You who are amorous and active, pause here an instant.
See passion transformed into rheumatism; rebellion into paralysis; power into a tumour.

That which was hated, became hateful; that which was crea-
tive, a stalking destruction; that which was loving, a tor-
menting flame
For those who reject their gifts: choose here their punishment.

Scene IV

(*Paradise Park. The operating theatre. Railed off, at the side
of the stage, are benches for students. Two* STUDENTS *are already seated there. The theatre itself is empty*)

1ST STUDENT   But surely you know that one?

2ND S.   Is it about the Italian and the two goats?

1ST S.   No, no. This is about a man who wanted to buy a
bird-cage. . . .
(*Whispers*)
          . . . He said: There's a stigma
          About the letter sigma. . . .

2ND S. (*laughing*)   That's damn good! Damn good, that is!
(ALAN *enters shyly and sits down in the corner, looking
round him*)

1ST S. (*indicating* ALAN)   Who's that johnny? Don't know
him.

2ND S.   A sweat-pot from one of the other hospitals, probably.

1ST S. (*to* ALAN)   Hullo. Are you from St. Gag's?

ALAN (*nervously*)   Er, yes.

1ST S.   What did you score this afternoon against Bullocks'?

2ND S.   Who's batting?

ALAN   Er, I think. . . .
(*At this moment, a* 3RD STUDENT *comes in. He is struggling
to get a white coat over his dinner-jacket*)

3RD S.   Thank God I'm not late! The old man had it in for
me today.

2ND S.   Hullo, Sandy. Were you at the Boat Club Supper?

3RD S.   Was I not! Just my luck to have to leave when things
were getting lively! They're just starting to wreck the hall.

Fatty's smashed his collar-bone already and Roy's lost a tooth. It's going to be a ripping rag.

1ST S.   Let's hope this case doesn't take long. (*Turning to* ALAN) By the way, what did you say the score was?

2ND S.   Ssh! They're coming!

(*An harmonium begins to play a voluntary. The* STUDENTS *and* ALAN *rise to their feet. Procession of* NURSES (*including* DOG), DRESSERS, *the* PATIENT *on the stretcher,* ANAESTHETIST *and* SURGEON. *The* SURGEON *takes up a position at the end of the table with his back to the audience. The note is given. ff subito. Flavour of Bach in his dramatic mood*)

ALL STUDENTS   (*heavy 4-part harmony*)
>   We see death every day
>   But do not understand him.

SUR.   I believe

ALL   in the physical causation of all phenomena, material or mental: and in the germ theory of disease. And in Hippocrates, the father of Medicine, Galen, Ambrose Paré, Liston of the enormous hands, Syme, Lister who discovered the use of antiseptics, Hunter and Sir Frederick Treves.

And I believe in surgical treatment for duodenal ulcer, cerebral abscess, pyloric stenosis, aneurism and all forms of endocrine disturbance.

SUR.   Let not the patient react unfavourably to the anaesthetic.

ALL   But let it save him from pain.

SUR.   Let there be no unforeseen complications.

ALL   Neither let sepsis have the advantage.

SUR.   May my skill not desert me.

ALL   But guide your hands.

SUR.   Gentlemen, we have before us a case of abdominal injury, caused by a bullet piercing the bowel. I intend there-fore to make a five-inch median incision, dividing the Rectus Abdominus, bring the bowel forward, resect it, wash out the peritoneum with warm saline and insert a tube for drainage. Is it clear?

ALL   It is.

(SURGEON *turns to wash his hands. During this process, the* STUDENTS *sing the following C of E, chant*)

DEC.   The surgeon is great: Let his name appear in the birth-day honours.

CAN.   I was in danger of death: And he delivered me.

DEC.   I was in fever and I could not sleep: The pain assailed me all day long.

CAN.   I groaned in the darkness: I was in terror for my life: I took no pleasure in women, neither in the innocent pastimes of children, my food had lost its flavour.

DEC.   The physicians shook their heads: they consulted together in the next room and were perplexed.

CAN.   They prescribed diets, cathartics, drugs and all manner of salves and ointments: but no one of them relieved me.

UNISON   But the surgeon, he relieved me: he removed the emphasis of my trouble and I was healed.

SURGEON   (*adjusting his gloves and picking up a scalpel*)   It's a terrible thing, nurse, to keep wicket for a man's life.

ALAN   Who's the surgeon?

1ST STUDENT   Sir William Spurgeon,
                The famous amateur cricketer:
                He captained the Hospital's team last year.

OTHER STUDENTS   Ssh!
    (*Roll of drums, as if before a tight-rope act in the circus. The* SURGEON *begins to operate. Suddenly the lights go out*)

SURGEON   Lights! Nurse! Dresser! You dresser next to that damned dresser! For God's sake get a torch! Light, give me a bloody light! Christ, is there no one in this bloody theatre who understands plain English? Someone go and find out what it's all about.
    (*Electric torches are brought. One of the* NURSES *goes out*)

SURGEON   Scalpel, nurse. Not that one, idiot! Forceps. More forceps! More! More! More!
    I have cut the mesenteric!
    Death has declared!
    (*Throws instruments about the room*)

ANAESTHETIST   He's sinking, sir. I'd better give him an injection of adrenalin.

SURGEON   (*to* DRESSER)   God man, don't chatter! Do something! How the Hell do you think I can see if you stand a mile away? Hold the torch nearer! Get out of my way!

SISTER   (*returning*)   It was the Boat Club, Sir William. They're having a supper tonight, you know. One of the students fused the lights. He says he's very sorry. They'll be on again in a few minutes.

SURGEON   Oh, he's sorry, is he? That's good. That's very good. I'll make him sorry he was ever born. I'll break him! I'll break the Hospital Boat! I'll have rowing forbidden in this Hospital for ever!

(*He utters a terrible roar and rushes out*)

3RD STUDENT   Just our luck! If it had been his precious cricketers, he'd have been as meek as a lamb.

A NURSE   Something's the matter. The patient's coming to! Holy Mother of all the Saints, have mercy!

(CHIMP EAGLE *sits up. The music of the ensuing duet should be in the style of Wagnerian opera*)

CHIMP   O Pressan Fells
  How beautiful you are!
I hear your bells
  Alas I cannot come
To Pressan home:
  I have wandered too far.

CHORUS   (Pain makes him wander in his mind,
There's nothing audible of any kind.)

ALAN   O my Eagle!

CHIMP   I hear a voice
  That makes me rejoice.
Who is it standing there?
  I cannot see you clear.

ALAN   Eagle, it is I,
  Alan Norman standing by.

CHIMP   I cannot see.
  Twixt you and me
Death's great tired face
  Hangs in space.

CHORUS   (Death makes him wander in his mind,
There's nothing visible of any kind.)

ALAN   I am near.
Do not fear.

CHIMP   She gives me loving glances.

ALAN   Where is Francis?

CHIMP   When the Midget died
I was by his side.

He said to me then
Out of his pain:
"Return again
To England. I swear
That Francis is there."
But I forgot
My choice and lot.
More I cannot tell.
Darkness assails me and I fail:
Farewell.

ALAN   O Eagle stay.
I will take you home.

CHIMP   Nay, death has come.
She beckons me away.
Beasts and flowers are in her keeping,
In her arms I would be sleeping.

ALAN   You shall not die!

CHIMP   No, Alan, no.
The surgeon now
Is ignorant as a dove.
To Iris my love.

(Dies)
(The lights go on again. The SURGEON *comes in)*

SUR.   That's settled 'em, I think. . . . Well, Sister, how's the patient?

SISTER   The patient is dead, Sir William.

SUR.   Dead! How dare you let him die? Great God, couldn't a dozen of you keep him alive for five minutes? This is the sort of thing which invariably happens whenever my back is turned. Typical. Typical. . . . What about this injection you gave the patient? Show me the bottle. (NURSE *gives it him*) And you can look me in the face and say you thought this was Adrenalin? Why, you blind miserable cow, this is hydrochloric acid!

SISTER *(in tears)*   The new probationer gave it me, Sir William.

SURGEON   The new probationer, eh? This is becoming amusing! Bring me the new probationer.
(The NURSES *push the* DOG *forward)*

SURGEON   So you're the culprit, eh? Well, let me tell you, my good girl, if I ever see you in this theatre again, I'll. . . .

(He becomes aware that he is staring into a DOG'S *face. There is an awful pause. The* SURGEON *makes some inarticulate sounds as if about to have a fit. The* DOG *utters a long-drawn howl. Then it turns and bolts for the door, its cap flying from its head. General dismay, confusion, screams, laughter, pursuit.* ALAN *rushes out after the others)*

CURTAIN

Scene V

(Night. The Highroad. In the middle of the stage stands a milestone)

CHORUS   Night. And crooked Europe hidden in shadow:
> The Rhine catching the moonlight for hundreds of miles, watched by lovers:
> Night in England: Over Lincolnshire and the great churches:
> Glimpses of the constellations between their pinnacles and flying buttresses:
> And here Alan and his companion, on foot on road, a forest on either side:
> A strong moon pitches their shadows forward:
> Sounds of their footsteps break against the woody masses
> But the tide in the tall trees is taciturn, another life:
> Alan lifting his eyes sees the Bear, the Waggoner, the Scales
> And Algol waxing and waning as his hope, no life at all.
> *(Enter* ALAN *and* DOG*)*

ALAN   Night has fallen, we have lost our way.
> You are tired and so am I.
> Let us wait till it is day.
> Against this milestone let us lie
> And sleep as best we may.
> *(They both lie down behind the milestone)*

CHORUS   Dear Sleep, the secretary of that strange club
> Where all are members upon one condition,
> That they forget their own importance;
> Where Lord and Link-Boy leave themselves with others
> And night after night for nothing are refreshed:
> May our names from your register never be struck off!
> *(Enter, from behind the milestone,* ALAN'S LEFT *and* RIGHT

FOOT. *The* RIGHT FOOT *speaks in a cultured voice, the* LEFT FOOT *has a Cockney accent)* *

RIGHT FOOT   Why are you pushing, Left?

LEFT F.   Cos yer tiking up all the room, that's why.

RIGHT F.   Well, that's no reason to push. Pushing won't make things better for either of us.

LEFT F.   It's bleedin' cold. Scratch me back for me, will yer, Right? Naow, a bit 'igher up.

RIGHT F.   Is that better?

LEFT F.   That's fine. Hell, I'm tired!

RIGHT F.   So am I. It's been a tiring day.

LEFT F.   I always feels tired now. Proper done in. The cramp keeps gettin' me. It gets me bad, sometimes.

RIGHT F.   You ought to see a doctor.

LEFT F.   Corse I ort. But the Boss won't let me. Jest let 'im wyte. One o' these dys I'll 'ave 'is guts fer garters.

RIGHT F.   I don't think you should talk like that, after all he's done for us.

LEFT F.   An' wot's 'e done fer us, I'd like ter know? Works us daown ter ther bone without so much as Thank You. And fer wot, I arsks yer? Fer wot? Chysin' abaht after some bloke wot's been dead fer years. A lot I care whether the Boss finds 'im. I 'aven't seen the inside of a carpet slipper fer weeks. Wot wouldn't I give fer a bath? Cor! I don't 'alf whistle!

RIGHT F.   Yes, the odour *is* unpleasant, certainly. Especially to feet like us, who've always been brought up to regard cleanliness as next to godliness. . . . Still, I must say, I don't see that grumbling does much good. And, look here, old chap, I do wish you wouldn't speak of the Master in that way. It makes such a bad impression when other people are about. Of course, I know you and I know quite well you don't mean a word of it. . . .

LEFT F.   Don't I, jest? That's all you knows! Look 'ere, wot'd you and yer precious Boss do if I was ter tell yer I wasn't goin' a step further? You'd 'ave ter carry me. 'Ow'd yer like that, eh?

* In a performance the ensuing dialogue should probably be cut.

RIGHT F. (*coldly*)   Of course, you're perfectly entitled to act as you think best. We can't stop you. I might just as well take the same attitude myself. . . . It's a matter of loyalty: either one appreciates that kind of thing, or one doesn't.

LEFT F.   You and yer Public School edjerkytion! Ort ter 'ave bin a sky pilot, you ort!

RIGHT F.   It's very easy to sneer. But the fact remains that without some kind of standards a fellow just goes to pieces. One saw enough of that in the War. Who were the best officers? The boys who had been captains of their school fifteens. And the more one knocks about the world, the more one comes to realise. . . .

LEFT F.   Ow, lay orf it! Yer mikes me sick! I ain't goin' ter listen ter another of yer lectures on the Team Spirit, an' that's stryte!

RIGHT F.   Sorry, old chap. I didn't mean to jaw. Let's change the subject, shall we? . . . You said just now that Sir Francis Crewe was dead. Well, I'm sure he's not. . . . And what's more, I'm on his track at last!

LEFT F.   Go on! You're kiddin'.

RIGHT F.   Oh no, I'm not. I'll prove it to you. I've been working on the case for months, now. I didn't want to say anything till I'd got it watertight. . . . And it's all so beautifully simple, really. . . . Do you know what gave me the first clue?

LEFT F.   Wot?

RIGHT F.   I happened to notice, one morning, that the Master's brown shoes had a little indentation on either side of the toe-cap, about half an inch long. At the time, I thought no more about it: It wasn't till the other day, fitting the facts together and trying them this way and that, that the whole thing flashed upon me. Do you know what had made those marks? (*Dramatically*) Roller-skates!

LEFT F.   But wot's that got ter do with Sir Francis Crewe?

RIGHT F.   I'll give you all the stages of my reasoning later: But it was really those skate-marks which led me to his hiding-place.

LEFT F.   Yer means you've seen 'im?

RIGHT F.   Oh no. I've never seen him yet. How could I? The Master never lets us go out alone.

LEFT F.   But yer knows where 'e is?

RIGHT F.   I do.

LEFT F.   Go on then, spit it aht!

RIGHT F.   (*impressively*)   At this very moment, Sir Francis
Crewe is . . . (*glances round him*) No. Better not tell you
here. There may be spies about. Come behind the milestone.
(*The* FEET *disappear*)

TWO CHORUS LEADERS

> Now through night's caressing grip
> Earth and all her oceans slip,
> Capes of China slide away
> From her fingers into day
> And the Americas incline
> Coasts towards her shadow line.
> Now the ragged vagrants creep
> Into crooked holes to sleep:
> Just and unjust, worst and best,
> Change their places as they rest:
> Awkward lovers lie in fields
> Where disdainful beauty yields:
> While the splendid and the proud
> Naked stand before the crowd
> And the losing gambler gains
> And the beggar entertains:
> May sleep's healing power extend
> Through these hours to our friend.
> Unpursued by hostile force,
> Traction engine, bull or horse
> Or revolting succubus;
> Calmly till the morning break
> Let him lie, then gently wake.

CURTAIN

Act Three

Chorus

A man and a dog are entering a city: They are approaching a
    centre of culture:
First the suburban dormitories spreading over fields,
Villas on vegetation like saxifrage on stone,
Isolated from each other like cases of fever
And uniform in design, uniform as nurses.
To each a lean-to shed, containing a well-oiled engine of es-
    cape.
Section these dwellings: expose the life of a people
Living by law and the length of a reference,
See love in its disguises and the losses of the heart,
Cats and old silver inspire heroic virtues
And psychic fields, accidentally generated, destroy whole fam-
    ilies.
Extraordinary tasks are set: a ploughman's hand acquires the
    most exquisite calligraphy,
A scheme is prepared for draining the North Sea, with the aid
    of books from the local library:
One has a vision in the bathroom after a family quarrel: he
    kneels on the cork mat:
A naturalist leaves in a cab in time for the breaking of the
    meres.
A youth with boils lies face down in bed, his mother over him;
Tenderly she squeezes from his trembling body the last dregs
    of his childhood.
Writer, be glib: please them with scenes of theatrical bliss and
    horror,
Whose own slight gestures tell their doom with a subtlety quite
    foreign to the stage.
For who dare patiently tell, tell of their sorrow

Without let or variation of season, streaming up in parallel
    from the little houses
And unabsorbed by their ironic treasures
Exerts on the rigid dome of the unpierced sky its enormous
    pressures?

But look: While we were talking, they have not stood still,
They have passed up the parade, the site of shops:
Goods are displayed: behind plate glass
One satin slipper austerely arranged
On an inky background of blackest velvet:
A waxen sandboy in skiing kit
Dumb and violet among vapour lamps.
High in the air, in empty space,
Five times a minute a mug is filled
And in ten-foot letters, time after time,
Words are spelt out and wiped away.
He moves amazed among the well-fed multitudes;
They glance at the stranger with the glance of those
Who have paid their allowance to be left alone.
And now they reach the Nineveh Hotel;
Consider this hotel: its appointments and fittings:
Five hundred bedrooms, with h and c,
Three hundred bathrooms: 375 W.Cs.:
Inspect the dining-hall: seating 2000:
The waiters scuttling from side to side
Like goldfish feeding the valuable people:
Admire the shining silver and cutlery
Stamped with the mark of that sombre town
Which fouls the Don still fresh from the moor
And the beautiful glassware blown on the Danube:
And stand in the vestibule spacious and gilded
As our hero enters to sign his name.
Old men afraid of reflections in glass
Are ushering ladies out to their cars,
Veiled and valued, through revolving doors.
Paid to be pretty, pumped into cloth,
Ranked by pillars pages wait,
At signals, like gulls from a nesting stack,
To rise on their toes and tear away.

Come in.

Scene I

(*The vestibule of the Nineveh Hotel.* PORTERS. PAGES. *Enter*
ALAN *and* DOG)

PORTER   I'm glad you've come, sir.
         You want a room, sir?

ALAN   Please.

PORTER   I'm sorry to be a trouble, sir:
         A single or a double, sir?

ALAN   A single, please.

PORTER   I'm still in doubt, sir.
         With bathroom or without, sir?

ALAN   With bathroom, please.

PORTER   Just sign your name, sir.
         And date the same, sir.
         Here, quickly, page boy.
         Or you'll put me in a rage, boy.
         Show this gentleman up to
         Room 132.

PAGE   Let me take your bag, sir.
         It'll save you fag, sir.
         Please follow me, sir.
         I've got the key, sir.

CHORUS   Make way, make way:
         This gentleman has come to stay.
         He wants a room where he may rest,
         But not the best, but not the best:
         He's only a provincial guest.

PORTER   (*sees* DOG)   I'm sorry, dogs are not allowed, sir,
         I didn't see him in the crowd, sir.

ALAN   But that's absurd, my dog and I
         Are never parted: tell me why,
         If not I'll give you back my keys
         And leave this moment, if you please!

(*Enter the* TWO JOURNALISTS. *The* 2ND JOURNALIST *is very drunk*)

2ND JOURNALIST (*singing*)
>   The bluebells bloomed on the Baltic shore
>   When Kit was Schneider-Creusot's love.

1ST J.   Why look, there's Alan!

2ND J.   My dear old boy!
>   To see you once more is indeed a joy!
(2ND J. *throws his arms round* ALAN'S *neck*)

1ST J.   He means no evil
>   But he's tight as the devil.

ALAN   I always hoped we should meet again.

1ST J.   What about your search? Has it been in vain?

ALAN   He never left England at all, it appears.

2ND J. (*who has wandered off into a corner, sings*)
>   Alice is gone and I'm alone,
>   Nobody understands
>   How lovely were her Fire Alarms,
>   How fair her German Bands!

1ST J. (*to* 2ND J.)   Stop! Stop! You make
>   My stomach ache!
>   (*To* ALAN)
>   Are you staying here?

ALAN   I'd hoped to. But they won't allow the dog.

1ST J.   They won't?
>   I'll settle that: You see if I don't!
>   Porter!

PORTER   What can I do, sir?
>   To satisfy you, sir?
>   (1ST J. *whispers something in his ear*)

PORTER   O O Sir,
>   I didn't know, sir!
>   (*To* ALAN)
>   I'm so sorry, sir.
>   I made a mistake, sir.
>   I was in a hurry, sir.
>   Don't worry, sir.
>   Of course we'll take, sir,
>   Your dog too, sir,
>   As well as you, sir.

(*To* PAGE)
> This dog you must take, boy,
> And feed on cake, boy.
(*Exeunt* PORTER, PAGE *and* DOG)

ALAN   Whatever did you say?

1ST J.   Ah, that's a secret I can't give away!
> Let's come and eat.

(*They go out.* 2ND J. *lingering behind, sings, out of tune and with great pathos*)

2ND J.   (*singing*)   O how I cried when Alice died
> The day we were to have wed!
> We never had our Roasted Duck
> And now she's a Loaf of Bread!

(*He staggers out*)

CURTAIN

Scene II

(*The restaurant of the Nineveh Hotel. In the foreground are tables with diners: including* ALAN *and the* TWO JOURNALISTS. *In the background is a small stage for cabaret. The entire setting of this scene should convey an impression of brutal, noisy vulgarity and tasteless extravagance. Band music*)

VOICES   And as for her hat, my dear . . .
> Le Touquet was lousy this year.
> Have you read *The Virgin Policeman?*
> Yes we did. We got right to the Docks.
> There's his new one.
> There were lots of children without any socks.
> You mean the blue one?
> It was divine. We found a dive.
> I'm flying next week to the Bahamas.
> And danced with the sailors. I felt so *alive*.
> What I say is: damn a man with holes in his pyjamas!
> Darling, you look wonderful tonight!
> One of those schools one has never heard of.

CABARET ANNOUNCER   Ladies and Gentlemen! The romance of foreign lands has been celebrated by every song-writer. But we feel that insufficient justice has been done to our

own country. We are presenting therefore to you tonight
Madame Bubbi, in a new song entitled: *Rhondda Moon*.
When you have heard her, I'm sure you will be convinced,
as we are, that, in the opportunities which she offers to the
Tender Passion, Britain is second to none! Madame Bubbi!
(*Enter* MADAME BUBBI, *an immense woman in a sequin
dress*)

M.B. (*sings*)
 I come with a message to the farmers and the cities;
 I've a simple slogan, it's just: Love British!
 British Romance, British joys,
 British chorus girls and chorus boys.

 The Sahara makes hearts go pit-a-pat,
 Glamorganshire can do better than that!
 Wherever you go, be it east or west,
 Remember British Love is quite the best.

 People sing songs about Tennessee
 But foreign men won't do for me.
 I don't want a dago, I don't want a Greek,
 I've got what I want and that's a British Sheik.

CHORUS On the Rhondda
 My time I squander
 Watching for my miner boy:
 He may be rough and tough
 But he surely is hot stuff
 And he's slender, to-me-tender,
 He's my only joy:
 Lovers' meeting,
 Lovers' greeting,
 O his arms will be around me soon!
 For I am growing fonder
 Out yonder as I wander
 And I ponder 'neath a Rhondda moon!

VOICES OF DINERS I bought five yards.
 I always use Corps de Femme myself.
 He's in the Guards.
 Oh, she's already on the shelf.
 I told him I couldn't do without it.
 Have you read *The Virgin Policeman?*
 The customs officer was perfectly sweet about it.
 (*Enter the* NINEVEH GIRLS. *All that is mechanical, shallow,
 silly, hideous and unbearably tragic in the antics of a modern*

cabaret chorus should be expressed here in its most exagger-
ated form. Crude lighting. Rowdy music)

NINEVEH GIRLS (*sing*)
　We are girls of different ages,
　All sorts of girls at all sorts of stages, we've
　　Come to delight you,
　　Come to excite you,
　　Come to present our revue!
　Fair girls, dear girls,
　Dark girls, stark girls,
　Glad girls, bad girls,
　Poor girls, we've-met-before-girls, we
　　All would welcome you.
　Desires, ambitions, anxieties fill us,
　We come from brick rectories and sham-Tudor villas,
　　It's our profession
　　To cure your depression
　　And banish those melancholy blues.
　Old girls, bold girls,
　Shy girls, fly girls,
　Kiss-girls, sis-girls,
　Lean girls, do-you-get-what-I-mean-girls, you
　　Only have to choose.
　We lift our legs for your masculine inspection,
　You can admire us without our correction, we
　　Do this nightly,
　　We hope we're not unsightly
　　Or all our labours are vain!
　Neat girls, sweet girls,
　Gym girls, slim girls,
　Meek girls, technique girls,
　Pat girls, come-up-to-my-flat-girls, we
　　Hope to see you again!
　(*Applause. A solitary* DINER *with an eye-glass beckons the*
　WAITER)

DINER　　Waiter!

WAITER　At once, sir!
　　　　You want, sir?

DINER　　Bring me the third girl from the right.
　　　　(*The* WAITER *blows a signal on his whistle and the chosen*
　　　　girl comes down from the stage. The WAITER *catches her*
　　　　head under his arm as though she were a fowl and holds her
　　　　so that the DINER *can pinch her thigh. The girl does not offer*
　　　　the least resistance)

WAITER   Will she do, sir?
Or will you choose anew, sir?

DINER   No. I'll have this one.

WAITER   Will you have her roast, sir,
Or on Japanese Toast, sir?
With Sauce Allemagne, sir,
Or stewed in white wine, sir?

DINER   Stewed, I think. But I'll have the finger-nails served
separately as a savoury. Oh, and don't forget to remind the
Chef to stir the pot with a sprig of rosemary. It makes all
the difference.
(WAITER *bows and retires, carrying the girl over his shoul-*
der)

CABARET ANNOUNCER   Our next item is Destructive Desmond!
(*Deafening applause.* DESTRUCTIVE DESMOND *comes on to*
the stage, followed by attendants carrying a large oil paint-
ing. DESMOND *is dressed as a schoolboy, with inkstains on*
his cheeks, a crumpled Eton collar, a striped cap, broken
bootlaces, dishevelled stockings and shorts. He is a stocky,
middle-aged man, with an inflamed, pugnacious face and
very hairy knees)

ONE OF THE DINERS TO ANOTHER   Haven't you seen him before? Oh, he's marvellous! I saw him last winter in New
York. He burnt an entire first folio Shakespeare, page by
page. I've never laughed so much in all my life.

DESMOND   Hullo, fellows! Here we are again! Has anyone got
a nice old poetry-book for me to read? I do love a bit of
poetry! (*Loud laughter from the audience*) You haven't?
Never mind! This evening, I've got a real treat for you. But,
first of all, is there any gentleman in the audience who knows
anything about painting? no, not painting the greenhouse.
(*Laughter*) Pictures! Come on, don't be shy. Thank you,
sir. Will you step up on the stage a moment?
(*An* ART EXPERT, *a nice, rather ineffective man in pince-nez,*
comes up. He is evidently a bona-fide member of the audi-
ence and not in the conspiracy. He does not at first under-
stand what is going to happen)

DESMOND (*winking at the audience*)   So you're an Art expert, sir?

ART EXPERT   Well, er, without wishing to be immodest, I
think I have some claim to that title, yes. I am the curator
of the gallery at Barchester.

DESMOND   Excellent! Just the man I wanted to meet! You see, sir, I wanted to ask your advice about a picture I've just bought. Would you care to look at it?

A.E. (*adjusting his pince-nez*)   Certainly, certainly. If I can be of any service. . . .
(DESMOND *signs to the attendants to uncover the picture. The* ART EXPERT *bends down to examine it. After a moment, he utters an exclamation, takes a magnifying glass from his pocket and studies every inch of the canvas with great care. The audience titters with delight: everybody else in the room seems to know exactly what will happen*)

A.E. (*standing up, evidently very much excited*)   Do you know, Mr. er Desmond . . . it's a very remarkable thing, very remarkable indeed . . . this picture is a Rembrandt!

DESMOND   Are you sure of that?

A.E.   Quite positive. There can be no doubt whatever.

DESMOND (*playing always to the audience, and mimicking the over-cultured tones of the* ART EXPERT)   No doubt whatever? Fancy that, now! And will you be so kind as to tell these ladies and gentlemen how much this Rembrandt of mine is worth?

A.E.   Oh, speaking offhand, I should say about sixty thousand pounds.

DESMOND (*as before*)   Isn't that a lot of money! Dear, Oh dear! And suppose something were to *happen* to my beautiful picture (*unseen by the* ART EXPERT, *but visible to the audience, he produces an enormous penknife: the audience are delighted*) do you think Mr. Rembrandt would paint me another one like it?

A.E. (*smiling*)   No, he couldn't, I'm afraid. He's dead.

DESMOND   Oh, he's dead, is he? I *am* sorry! I must send some flowers. What did he die of?
(*The* ART EXPERT *doesn't quite know what to make of this fooling. He has become aware of the curiously hostile mood of* DESMOND *and the audience towards himself. He stands there awkwardly, smiling but uneasy*)

DESMOND   Well, well (*he flourishes the knife*) if Mr. Rembrandt's dead, he won't be angry with me: that's one comfort. And anyhow, I suppose I can do what I like with my own picture. . . .

A.E. (*suddenly realising what* DESMOND *is going to do*)   Mr.
Desmond! . . . You're not going to . . . ?

DESMOND   Not going to what?

A.E. (*gasping*)   To . . . destroy this picture?

DESMOND (*now openly sneering at him*)   And why shouldn't
I destroy it, may I ask? Isn't it mine?

A.E.   . . . Yes, er, of course. . . . But I mean. . . . You
can't . . . it's a masterpiece!

DESMOND   Oh, it's a masterpiece, is it? And how would you
define a masterpiece, Mr. Art Expert?

A.E.   Something unique . . . a work of genius . . . which
can't be replaced . . . priceless . . . (*he stammers, amidst
the merriment of the audience, and cannot go on*)

DESMOND (*signs to the attendants to uncover a second picture*)   Is *this* a masterpiece?

A.E. (*contemptuously*)   No, most certainly not!

DESMOND   Why isn't it?

A.E.   In the first place because it's a completely tasteless piece
of third-rate Victorian landscape painting of which you'll
find examples in every boarding-house in England: And
secondly, because it isn't even an original. You could get
as many copies as you wanted from the publishers for a
shilling a piece.

DESMOND   Well, all I can say is: I think it's a very nice picture. I like it much better than Mr. Rembrandt's, which you
say is so valuable. (*Pointing to the Rembrandt*) Why, this
is all *brown!* More like a chest of drawers! Ugh, how I hate
you!
(*Raises knife to slash the Rembrandt canvas*)

A.E. (*almost in tears*)   Stop! I protest against this disgraceful
exhibition! I appeal to the ladies and gentlemen of the audience. Surely you won't allow this to go on?

DESMOND   Aha! So you appeal to the audience, do you? Very
well! (*To the audience*) Ladies and gentlemen, I leave it
entirely in your hands: which picture would you rather see
cut to bits, this landscape which Mr. Expert so much despises, or old mahogany Rembrandt?

ALL THE DINERS   Rembrandt! Rembrandt!

DESMOND (*brutally, to* ART EXPERT)   You hear what they

say? And now, get off my platform! If you don't like it, you can do the other thing!

A.E. (*putting his hands to his head*) Either these people are mad, or I am! (*He jumps down from the stage and runs out of the restaurant*)

(DESMOND *waves an ironic goodbye after him. The drums begin to roll. The audience groan with delight.* DESMOND, *standing before the Rembrandt, works himself up into a state of hysterical fury. He makes faces at the canvas, shows his teeth, shakes his fist, spits*)

DESMOND (*As the drums reach their climax*) Grrrr! Take that, you brute! (*slashes canvas with his knife*) and that! and that!

(*Finale of trumpets. The attendants hold up the slashed picture and* DESMOND *puts his arm through it several times. Then he strikes it from their hands and tramples on it on the floor. Terrific applause.* DESMOND *bows and exits*)
(*A trumpet*)

A VOICE Here comes Miss Lou Vipond,
The star of whom the world is fond!
(*All the diners jump up and rush towards the entrance, to get a peep.* ALAN *is one of the first. As* MISS VIPOND *passes across the stage, she is completely hidden by the crowd*)

1ST JOURNALIST
Alan, old boy, come back! come back!
Don't you cross that harpy's track!

2ND J. If you fall for that dame, it'll be your undoing:
She's brought enough good men to their ruin.

ALAN (*who is standing on a table in order to see better*)
You fellows talk the most utter rot!
All other women can go to pot!
I'm true to Iris.
(*He catches sight of* MISS VIPOND)
By Jove, she's a stunner!
What a face! I'm dazzled!
(*He jumps down from his table into the middle of the crowd*)

1ST J. (*covering his eyes*) The kid's a goner!

VOICES FROM THE CROWD ROUND ALAN
She's stopped to speak to a stranger!
Then he's in danger!
Look at her eyes!

What a lovely surprise!
She pretends she feels tired!
O she's inspired!
She leans on his arm!
She knows her charm!
She's going to speak!
It makes his knees weak!
She has asked him to visit her room!
He goes to his doom!

(ALAN, *his face transformed by joy, breaks through the crowd and rushes forward*)

ALAN (*to* JOURNALISTS)
Where can I get some flowers
So long after hours?

(*Without waiting for an answer, he runs out*)

CHORUS   Inform the Press, inform the Press,
Miss Vipond's had one more success!
It's in the air, it's in the air,
She's going to have a new affair!

Make way, make way,
This gentleman has come to stay!
He wants the best, he wants the best,
He's more than a provincial guest!

He quickly fell, he quickly fell,
He lost his heart in our hotel!
He's going to start, he's going to start,
He's starting now to break his heart!

CURTAIN

Scene III

(*Before the curtain. Enter simultaneously* ALAN, *left, and the* DOG, *right. They meet in the middle of the stage.* ALAN *is in tails. He carries an immense bouquet of flowers*)

ALAN (*in a great hurry*)   Hullo, Doggy! How's life? (*The* DOG *fawns on him*) Not now, there's a good dog! I'm in an awful hurry. Just think, in another minute I shall be with her! I believe, if I didn't see her again, I should go crazy!

But you can't understand that, can you, Doggy? As long as you get your food and a nice warm mat to lie on, you're perfectly happy. I wish I were a dog! No, I'm damn glad I'm not. (*He pats the* DOG's *head absentmindedly*) Well, I must be off. (*The* DOG *puts its paws on* ALAN's *shoulders*) Here, I say! That's enough! Let me alone, can't you? What's the matter with you this evening? Down, sir! (*He pushes the* DOG *roughly aside*) Now you've made my coat dirty. I shall have to get it brushed. Silly fool! (*He takes a step forward. Immediately, the* DOG *jumps up and drags the flowers from his hand, scattering them in all directions*) Francis, how dare you! You clumsy brute! (ALAN *gives the* DOG *a kick*) Get out! (*The* DOG *does not move. There is a pause*) I say, Francis, old boy, I didn't mean to do that! Honestly I didn't! I've never kicked you before, have I? You just made me angry with you for the moment. I'm sorry. . . . Why do you look at me like that? You can't pretend I really hurt you: Now, can you? Let me see. . . . (*He moves his hand towards the* DOG. *The* DOG *retreats a little*) Oh, very well, if you'd rather not. Here: Shake a paw! (*The* DOG *does not move*) All right, then: sulk if you want to. I've said I'm sorry. I can't do any more, can I? And anyhow, it was all your fault. (*Pointing to the flowers*) Just look at them: all ruined! Now I shall have to get some more, and they cost five shillings each. What made you do it, Francis? Ha ha ha! I believe you're jealous again! Was that why? Well, you are a queer dog! But you wait till you see her, Francis. She's the most marvellous creature in the world! Goodness knows what she can see in a chap like me! Her eyes, why, you've no idea. . . . (*But the* DOG *has turned and, with great dignity, slowly walked off the stage*) He's gone! Funny! I expect he'll be all right tomorrow. . . . And now! (ALAN *straightens his coat and smooths his hair*) I must get those flowers. (*Looks at his watch*) Good God! I'm five seconds late already!

(*He rushes out*)

Scene IV

(*The Nineveh Hotel. The stage is divided in half. The right-hand scene represents* MISS VIPOND's *bedroom. The left-hand scene is the corridor outside it. When the curtain rises, the*

bedroom is in darkness. The corridor is illuminated. The DOG
*is sitting on a chest outside the bedroom door. A grandfather
clock stands in the corner. Enter the* MANAGER, *with a chorus
of* WAITERS, PAGES *and* CHAMBERMAIDS)

MANAGER When he gets his bill tomorrow
    What will Mr. Norman say?
   Will he shoot himself for sorrow
    All on a summer's day?

CHORUS Perhaps he'll only lose his mind,
    Go wild and feed among the lilies:
   Tell us, if you'd be so kind,
    Tell us what the bill is.

MANAGER 20 cases of champagne,
   A finest pedigree Great Dane,
   Half a dozen Paris frocks,
   A sable fur, a silver fox,
   Bottles of scent and beauty salves,
   An MG Midget with overhead valves,
   1 doz pairs of shoes and boots,
   6 lounge, 1 tails and 3 dress suits,
   A handsome two-piece bathing-dress,
   An electric razor, a trouser-press,
   A cutter for cigars, two lighters,
   10 autographs of famous writers,
   Berths and tickets in advance
   For a trip round Southern France:
   Add to this his bed and board.

CHORUS It's more than one man can afford.

MANAGER This we'll keep until the morning.
   Remember, do not give him warning.
  (*Exit*)
  (*Song and Step Dance*)

WAITERS If we're late
   Or break a plate
   He won't be rude.
   If we served him nude
   Would he know?
   No No No!
   He's in love!

PAGES If we lose
   All his shoes,
   Say Go to Hell

When he rings the bell,
He won't know:
No No No!
He's in love!

CHAMBERMAID   If I stops
Emptying the slops,
Leaves a dead
Mouse in the bed,
He won't know:
No No No!
He's in love!

(*A bell rings. The* CHORUS *arrange themselves under the* HEAD WAITER)

HEAD WAITER
The Nineveh Hotel holds the copyright
Of the Epithalamium we are going to recite.

CHORUS (*reciting, with a background of eighteeenth-century music*)
You who return tonight to a narrow bed
With one name running sorrowfully through your sorrowful head,
You who have never been touched, and you, pale lover,
Who left the house this morning kissed all over,
You little boys also of quite fourteen
Beginning to realise just what we mean,
Fill up glasses with champagne and drink again.

It's not a new school or factory to which we summon,
We're here today because of a man and a woman.
Oh Chef, employ your continental arts
To celebrate the union of two loving hearts!
Waiters, be deft, and slip, you pages, by
To honour the god to name whom is to lie:
Fill up glasses with champagne and drink again.
(*The corridor begins to darken*)
Already he has brought the swallows past the Scillies
To chase each other skimming under English bridges,
Has loosed the urgent pollen on the glittering country
To find the pistil, force its burglar's entry,
He moves us also and up the marble stair
He leads the figures matched in beauty and desire:
Fill up glasses with champagne and drink again.
(*The corridor is now completely dark.* MISS VIPOND's *bedroom is illuminated.* ALAN *stands embracing* MISS VIPOND,

*who is a shopwindow dummy, very beautifully dressed.
When the dummy is to speak,* ALAN *runs behind it and
speaks in falsetto*)

ALAN

My swan, so beautiful to my five senses,
When I look on you, in a moment I lose my defences,
My clumsy heart forgets herself and dances.

DUMMY

O lion, O sun, encompass me with power,
Feed lion, shine sun, for in your glory I flower,
Create the huge and gorgeous summer in an hour.

VOICES OF WAITERS' CHORUS (*outside in the corridor*)
What would you give that she might live?

ALAN

I would give the Netherlands with all their canals,
The earth of the Ukraine, the Niagara Falls,
The Eiffel Tower also and the Dome of St. Paul's.

CHORUS OUTSIDE
What would you do to keep her true?

ALAN

I would hunt the enormous whale in the Arctic lowlands,
I would count all the starlings in the British Islands,
I would run through fighting Europe in absolute silence.

DUMMY

But men are treacherous, I know, as the North-East wind,
They speak of loving but another is in their mind,
And you will leave me tomorrow morning for another find.

ALAN

True, there was one I thought I loved beyond measure.
Here is her picture, I destroy it to give you pleasure.
For, love, in your arms I find the only treasure.
(*He tears up the photograph of* IRIS *and scatters the pieces
at the dummy's feet*)

DUMMY

Our sails are set. O launch upon love's ocean,
Fear has no means there of locomotion
And death cannot exhaust us with his endless devotion.
(ALAN *begins to embrace and undress the dummy. The bedroom slowly darkens. From the complete darkness of the
corridor, the voices of the* WAITERS' CHORUS *are heard, gradually receding*)

CHORUS
It's not only this we praise, it's the general love:
Let cat's mew rise to a scream on the tool-shed roof,
Let son come home tonight to his anxious mother,
Let the vicar lead the choirboy into a dark corner.
The orchard shall flower tonight that flowers every hundred
    years,
The boots and the slavey be found dutch-kissing on the
    stairs:
Fill up glasses with champagne and drink again.

Let this be kept as a generous hour by all,
This once let the uncle settle his nephew's bill,
Let the nervous lady's table gaucheness be forgiven,
Let the thief's explanation of the theft be taken,
The boy caught smoking shall escape the usual whipping,
Tonight the expensive whore shall give herself for nothing:
Fill up glasses with champagne and drink again.

The landlocked state shall get its port today,
The midnight worker in the laboratory by the sea
Shall discover under the cross-wires that which he looks for,
Tonight the asthmatic clerk shall dream he's a boxer,
Let the cold heart's wish be granted, the desire for a desire,
O give to the coward now his hour of power:
Fill up glasses with champagne and drink again.
(*The bedroom is now completely dark. In the corridor, spot-
lights suddenly illuminate the chest and the grandfather
clock. Beside the chest the* DOG *is lying with its paws
crossed*)

DOG'S SKIN Ticker! Ticker! Are you awake? (*The Clock
strikes one*) It's only me, the dog's skin that hides that eccentric young man. I hope you admire my accent? I've lived
so long with them, I have all the émigré's pride, at having
forgotten my own. I'm quite déraciné, as they say in Blooms-
bury. When I first paid them a visit, before I gave up my
nationality and was still an Irish Wolfhound, I was very
romantic. The odour of a particular arm-chair, the touch of
certain fingers, excited me to rash generalisations which I
believed to be profound. I composed poems that I imagined
highly idiomatic, on the words "walk" and "dinner." And it
was in this romantic mood that I decided to throw in my
lot with theirs and sever all ties with my past. My dearest
ambition was to be accepted naturally as one of them. I was

soon disillusioned! To them I was only a skin, valued for
its associations with that very life I had hoped to abandon.
Small children misunderstood by their parents rubbed tear-
ful cheeks against me and whispered secrets to their doggie.
I ask you . . . Doggie! Young men wore me at charades
to arouse in others undisguised human amusement and desire. Talking about charades, Ticker, are you interested in
literature at all? (*The Clock strikes two*) You are? So am I.

In the old days, before I became a skin, I used to be the
pet of a very famous author. He talked all day to yours
truly. He suffered terribly from indigestion, poor fellow, and
wrote what was called "virile" poetry. He was knighted for
it during the War. Well, I'll tell you a story about him. One
night (it was nearly one o'clock in the morning, as a
matter of fact) he was pretty tight on whisky and we had
a real heart-to-heart. George, he says (I was called George
in those days), George, he says, come here. I came, rather
crossly, to tell you the truth, I was sleepy and wishing he'd
go to bed. George, look at me. Do I make you sick? (By the
way, I forgot to tell you that it was during the War, at the
time of the big German offensive in March of '18.) Less
than a hundred miles from here, young men are being
blown to pieces. Listen, you can hear the guns doing it. (It
was quite true, you could. We lived on the South Downs
and it was a still night.) Every time I hear that, I say to
myself: You fired that shell. It isn't the cold general on his
white horse, nor the owner of the huge factory, nor the
luckless poor, but you. Yes, I and those like me. Invalid
poets with a fountain pen, undersized professors in a class-
room, we, the sedentary and learned, whose schooling cost
the most, the least conspicuous of them all, are the assassins.
(I'm giving you his own words. Whisky always made him a
bit rhetorical.) We have conjured up all the vigours and all
the splendours, skilfully transferred our envy into an image
of the universal mother, for which the lad of seventeen whom
we have always sent and will send again against our terrors,
gladly immolates himself. Men are falling through the air in
flames and choking slowly in the dark recesses of the sea to
assuage our pride. Our pride! Who cannot work without
incessant cups of tea, spend whole days weeping in our
rooms, immoderately desire little girls on beaches and buy
them sweets, cannot pass a mirror without staring, for whom
a slight cold is enough to create a day-dream of our death-
bed with appropriate organ-music. . . . Now wasn't that
queer? It was the last talk I ever had with him. He couldn't

bear the sight of me after that evening and sold me as soon as he could.

Just like a man! You know, Ticker, I think the important thing to remember about Man is that pictures mean more to him than people. Take sex, for instance. Well, you've seen what it was like this evening. Sometimes it's funny and sometimes it's sad, but it's always hanging about like a smell of drains. Too many ideas in their heads! To them I'm an idea, you're an idea, everything's an idea. That's why we're here. Funny thing, Ticker, that we should both be in the same play. They can't do without us. If it wasn't for me, this young man of mine would never be able to get a good night's rest: and if it wasn't for you he'd never wake up. And look what we do to the audience! When I come on, they start sighing, thinking of spring, meadows and goodness knows what else: While you make them demand a tragic ending, with you they associate an immensely complicated system of awards and punishments. (*During this speech, the corridor has been gradually illuminated*)

Heavens. It's getting light and you've forgotten to strike! Hurry up! (*The Clock strikes six*) I think someone's coming and my lodger is waking up. So long! Abyssinia.

(*The* DOG *stretches.* FRANCIS CREWE *gets out of the skin, lays it on the chest, looks cautiously round and tip-toes out*)

(MANAGER, WAITERS, PAGES, *etc. enter singing—Air: John Peel*)

MANAGER

The sun has risen and it shines through the blind,
This lover must awaken and recall to mind
Though the pillow be soft and the lady be kind,
Yet the man has to pay in the morning.

CHORUS   For in Nineveh Hotel the most humble guest,
Be he old, be he young, he may take a good rest,
He may smoke cigars, he may order the best,
But we hand him the bill in the morning.

(*The* MANAGER *knocks loudly at the bedroom door.* ALAN *appears in pyjamas*)

ALAN   What's all this row,
            I can't see you now?

CHORUS   We're sorry, sir,
            To be a worry, sir,
            But we're in a hurry, sir.
            We want our money, sir.
            Here is our bill, sir.

(*They give him the bill. Pause*)
      Oh, don't be ill, sir!

ALAN   Fifteen hundred! It's absurd!
      This will have to be deferred.
      I'm sorry, gentlemen, to say
      Just at this moment I cannot pay.
      You shall have your money another day.

CHORUS   Till we have our due, we stay.

ALAN   Here's a to-do!
      I must borrow from Lou.
(*He speaks into the bedroom, which is in darkness*)
      Darling, I'm sorry to be such a bother
      But some stupid tradesman is making a pother
      (It's nothing really) about my account:
      So will you lend it me, darling Lou?
      Fifteen hundred pounds will do.
(*No answer*)
      Darling, please,
      Don't be a tease,
      They're waiting here,
      They will fetch the Police.
      Please be a dear!
(*No answer*)
      Say something, do!
      I want help, Lou!
(*No answer*)
      Why don't you answer?
      I tell you, I'm in danger!
(*No answer*)
      Last night you spoke.
      This is no joke!
(*No answer*)
      What is the matter, what have I done?
      Last night you called me your lion and your sun
      Speak to me, please, just one little word,
      I don't understand you! Oh, this is absurd!
(*A pause*)
      I am your lover!
      Don't say that's over!
      That can't be what you mean!
(*A pause*)
      I won't believe it!
(*A pause*)
      All right, I'll leave it.

Oh, I'm in hell!
(*He turns to the* MANAGER *and others outside in the corridor*)

MANAGER   Well?

ALAN   Gentlemen, what can I say?
I cannot pay!

MANAGER   This is a most regrettable occasion.
I must go at once to the police station.
Alphonse.

ALPHONSE   Yes sah?

MANAGER   Tell the Porter he's not to let
This man go out: and don't forget!
(*Exeunt* MANAGER *and others*)

ALAN   Lou! Lou!
There is only one thing left to do,
Something that the Romans knew,
In a bath I'll open a vein
And end my life with little pain.
I'll go at once and turn
The water on and then return
For the razor to relieve
Me for ever of my grief.

(*He enters the darkened bedroom and disappears.* FRANCIS CREWE *comes into the corridor, takes the skin from the chest and hastily begins getting into it. While he is doing so,* ALAN *reappears at the bedroom door*)

ALAN   What are you doing to my dog? You've killed him? Oh this is the end of everything!

FRANCIS   Alan!

ALAN   You know my name? Who are you? What do you want?

FRANCIS   I ought to know your name by this time. I've been with you long enough.

ALAN   My Goodness! You don't mean . . . ?

FRANCIS   Yes, I'm your faithful doggy. This is how I look in mufti. But you can go on calling me Francis. It's my real name.

ALAN   My God, who are you? You're not . . . ?

FRANCIS   (*mimicking* ALAN'S *voice*)
        "Is the name Sir Francis Crewe,
            English, known perhaps to you?"

ALAN   Francis! At last! (*They embrace*) Oh, this is the happiest moment of my life! Everything's all right now!

FRANCIS   I'm glad you think so.

ALAN   Well, isn't it?

FRANCIS   (*nodding towards the bedroom door*)   What about
Miss Vipond?

ALAN   Oh, that's all over. I was mad, I think. She's the most
utter bitch.

FRANCIS   I could have told you that.

ALAN   (*laughing*)   You did try to, didn't you? I say, Francis,
I'm most awfully sorry I kicked you.

FRANCIS   That's all right. It was my fault, really. My attempts
at dissuasion were somewhat crude. You've no idea what
self-control it took not to answer you back, though. You'd
have got a shock if the dog had spoken!

ALAN   Yes, shouldn't I . . . I say, Francis, there's so much I
want to ask you, I don't know where to begin! Whatever
made you dress up as a dog, at all?

FRANCIS   I'll tell you all about that, but not now. The first
question is, what are we going to do?

ALAN   Well . . . go back to Pressan Ambo, of course.

FRANCIS   You really want to?

ALAN   Of course I want to.

FRANCIS   And marry my charming sister?

ALAN   Yes . . . rather!

FRANCIS   You don't sound quite so enthusiastic as you were.
Still, a promise is a promise, isn't it? Let's hope it won't be
broken. . . . You're longing to be back in Pressan again, I
suppose? You know, you may find it rather changed.

ALAN   Rot! Dear old Pressan will never change.

FRANCIS   Places sometimes look different when one comes
back to them. . . . However, we'll go there together and
you shall judge for yourself.

ALAN   That's ripping! My word, won't they be delighted to see
you!

FRANCIS   Yes, I can just picture Hotham's face; streaming
with tears of joy. And the dear Vicar.

ALAN   You sound as if you didn't like them much.

FRANCIS   Perhaps I don't.

ALAN   What a queer sort of chap you are, Francis! I can't make you out at all. You're not a bit like I imagined you would be. . . . You must have led a funny sort of life, all these years. Did you often go out by yourself, like last night?

FRANCIS   Not often, no. I had to be very careful. The last few weeks I've been more reckless, because I knew you'd catch me sooner or later. In fact, I was considering whether I oughtn't to reveal myself. It was selfish of me not to, I know; but I've enjoyed our trip so much I didn't want it to end. . . . That reminds me, here are your shoes. I always had to borrow them. You can't wear shoes in this skin, you see.

VOICES OF THE WAITERS *are heard singing, off*
For in Nineveh Hotel the most humble guest . . . *etc.*

ALAN   Great God! I quite forgot! Francis, I'm in the most awful fix! They're coming to arrest me for not paying my bill. Whatever shall I do?

FRANCIS   Don't worry. I'd thought of that. Here, get into the dog's skin. I'll manage the rest.
(*He helps* ALAN *to put on the dog's skin. Enter the* MANAGER, *with* POLICEMEN, WAITERS, *etc.*)

FRANCIS   Waiter, I've lost my way. How do I get to the Roof Garden?

WAITER   Take the lift on the right, sir.
At the Fifth you alight, sir.
(*Bows*)

MANAGER (*seeing* DOG)   That ugly brute!
I've an itch in my foot!
(*Kicks it*)
This is the door, officer.

ALAN (*rubbing himself with his paw, in a low voice to* FRANCIS)   The swine!

FRANCIS   Ha ha! Now you know how it feels!

POLICE SERGEANT (*at bedroom door*)
Open this door
In the name of the Law!
(*Knocks*)

FRANCIS (*in a low voice to* ALAN)   We'll try and find your two journalist friends and take them with us to Pressan. They may as well see how this business ends.

(*Exeunt* FRANCIS *and* ALAN)
(*The* MANAGER, WAITERS, POLICEMEN *all stand round the door. The* POLICEMAN *knocks for the second time*)

CURTAIN

Chorus

So, under the local images your blood has conjured,
We show you man caught in the trap of his terror, destroying
    himself.
From his favourite pool between the yew-hedge and the roses,
    it is no fairy-tale his line catches
But grey, white and horrid, the monster of his childhood raises
    its huge domed forehead
And death moves in to take his inner luck,
Lands on the beaches of his love, like Coghlan's coffin.

Do not speak of a change of heart, meaning five hundred a
    year and a room of one's own,
As if that were all that is necessary. In these islands alone there
    are some forty-seven million hearts, each of four cham-
    bers:
You cannot avoid the issue by becoming simply a community
    digger,
O you who prattle about the wonderful Middle Ages: You who
    expect the millennium after a few trifling adjustments.

Visit from house to house, from country to country: consider
    the populations
Beneath the communions and the coiffures: discover your im-
    age.
Man divided always and restless always: afraid and unable to
    forgive:
Unable to forgive his parents, or his first voluptuous rectal
    sins,
Afraid of the clock, afraid of catching his neighbour's cold,
    afraid of his own body,
Desperately anxious about his health and his position: calling
    upon the Universe to justify his existence,
Slovenly in posture and thinking: the greater part of the will
    devoted

To warding off pain from the water-logged areas,
An isolated bundle of nerve and desire, suffering alone,
Seeing others only in reference to himself: as a long-lost
    mother or as his ideal self at sixteen.

Watch him asleep and waking:
Dreaming of continuous sexual enjoyment or perpetual ap-
    plause;
Reading of accidents over the breakfast-table, thinking: "This
    could never happen to me."
Reading the reports of trials, flushed at the downfall of a fel-
    low creature.
Examine his satisfactions:
Some turn to the time-honoured solutions of sickness and
    crime: some to the latest model of aeroplane or the sport
    of the moment.
Some to good works, to a mechanical ritual of giving.
Some have adopted an irrefragable system of beliefs or a po-
    litical programme, others have escaped to the ascetic
    mountains
Or taken refuge in the family circle, among the boys on the
    bar-stools, on the small uncritical islands.
Men will profess devotion to almost anything; to God, to Hu-
    manity, to Truth, to Beauty: but their first thought on
    meeting is: "Beware!"
They put their trust in Reason or the Feelings of the Blood,
    but they will not trust a stranger with half-a-crown.
Beware of those with no obvious vices; of the chaste, the non-
    smoker and drinker, the vegetarian:
Beware of those who show no inclination towards making
    money: there are even less innocent forms of power.
Beware of yourself:
Have you not heard your own heart whisper: "I am the nicest
    person in this room"?
Asking to be introduced to someone "real": someone unlike all
    those people over there?

You have wonderful hospitals and a few good schools:
Repent.
The precision of your instruments and the skill of your design-
    ers is unparalleled:
Unite.
Your knowledge and your power are capable of infinite ex-
    tension:
Act.

Scene V

(*As in Act I, Scene I: The Garden of the Vicarage at Pressan Ambo. A platform, draped with the Union Jack, occupies most of the stage. On it are chairs, a table and a glass of water. Other chairs are arranged round the platform, in preparation for a meeting. Two large banners are hung right across the stage. They are inscribed: "The Lads of Pressan teach Britain a lesson" and "Pressan is having breakfast: Wake up, England!" Many other flags, Scottish, Welsh, Irish and Colonial, hang down from the branches of the trees. As the curtain rises, the stage is empty. Enter* ALAN, FRANCIS *and the* TWO JOURNALISTS. FRANCIS *wears the dog's skin, but with the head thrown back, like a monk's cowl. He walks on his feet: not on all fours. The* JOURNALISTS *carry cameras and other photographic apparatus*)

ALAN (*looking about him in amazement*)   Whatever can have happened? I say, Francis, do you think they can have found out that we were coming?

FRANCIS   On the contrary: I should say that today of all others is the day on which they least expect to see us.

1ST JOURNALIST   Well, Alan, your native hamlet certainly seems to be moving with the times. From your description, I was expecting an oldest inhabitant and a prize pig.

2ND J.   The last of my illusions is shattered. So this is rural England! Just another lousy racket!

ALAN   But I tell you, it never used to be like this. I simply can't understand it. Everything's different! (*He looks off-stage, through the trees*) I say, here comes the Curate. He'll be able to tell us what's up.

FRANCIS   No. I don't want him to see us, yet. (*To the* JOURNALISTS) You two can question him. Come along, Alan. We'll go down there, where we can watch.
(*He and* ALAN *descend into the auditorium and take seats among the audience. Enter the* CURATE)

JOURNALISTS (*raising their hats*)   Good day, sir. *The Thunderbolt. The Evening Moon.* Perhaps you'd care to tell us something about your interesting celebrations? We're very anxious to get the details correct. Nothing shall be printed without your approval. The articles will be ready for your O.K. before we leave here this afternoon.

CURATE (*who is evidently overworked and disgusted; finding the whole subject extremely distasteful*)   I'm not authorized to give you any information. You ought to speak to the Vicar, really: but he's very busy just now. (*Sighs and passes his hand over his eyes*) Oh, very well, what is it you want to know?

(*The* JOURNALISTS *take out their notebooks*)

1ST J.   My colleague and myself very much appreciate your kindness, sir. We won't take up more of your valuable time than is absolutely necessary. . . . Who exactly, are the Lads of Pressan?

CURATE (*as if wearily repeating a lesson he has learnt*)   The Lads of Pressan is a Boys' Brigade founded by the Vicar and General Hotham. Miss Iris Crewe is Patroness and Mrs. Hotham Honorary Colonel-in-Chief. The uniforms have been designed by the Vicar. Today, the Brigade is to have its first inspection by General and Mrs. Hotham. The Vicar will preach a sermon on Bolshevism and the Devil. And Miss Iris Crewe will present the Standard, which will then be blessed by the Vicar. Later, there will be Field Communion, tea and athletic sports.

2ND J.   Very interesting. . . . And what are the objects of this Brigade?

CURATE   Well, er. . . . The Vicar says . . . you see. . . . (*This subject is evidently so repugnant to him that he can hardly force himself to begin*)

1ST J. (*helpfully*)   "Standing outside all political parties and factions, for Church, King and State, against communism, terrorism, pacifism and other forms of international anarchy, to protect Religion and succour England in times of national crisis." Is that right, sir?

CURATE (*surprised*)   Why, those are almost exactly the Vicar's own words? However did you know?

2ND J.   It's the usual, er . . . programme. Thank you very much, sir. And now, if you'll be kind enough to show us the Press places, we won't keep you any longer.

CURATE   I should think you'd see best over there.

(*He indicates two chairs in a corner, at the front of the*

stage. The JOURNALISTS *go over to them and take their seats*)

(*Band music, of a military character, can already be heard off. Enter the* VICAR, *fussily, in a bad temper. He wears his cassock and surplice*)

VICAR (*to* CURATE)   Ah, here you are! Whatever have you been doing? I've been looking for you everywhere. Do you expect me to attend to everything myself?

CURATE   I'm very sorry.

VICAR   It's very easy to say you're sorry. But you don't do much to show it. This is the third time I've had to reprove you this week! You seem to have no life in you, no go, no enthusiasm. I'm beginning to be very much afraid that your heart isn't in our movement!

CURATE   You're quite right, sir. It's no good our going on like this: I'd better tell you frankly. . . .

(*The band, which has been getting louder, now blares out just behind the scenes*)

THE VICAR   Good Gracious! Here they are!

(*He runs out, to meet the others; returning almost immediately with the* GENERAL, MRS. HOTHAM *and* MISS IRIS CREWE. *These four take their places on the raised platform. Crowds of villagers enter and sit down on the chairs on the stage. Finally, the Lads of Pressan, wearing a distinctive uniform, march in and form ranks just below the platform. A boy with the standard which* MISS IRIS CREWE *is later to present takes his place on the platform behind her chair. The chatter of the villagers is drowned by the noise of the band*)

(*The military music ends with a flourish. Silence. The* VICAR *rises to his feet. He delivers the following sermon: beginning in his usual pulpit manner, but quickly becoming more excited, more histrionic, more daring in his gestures and poses. The final passage is wailed rather than spoken. Tears pour down his cheeks, saliva runs from his mouth: He has worked himself up into an hysterical frenzy*)

VICAR   What was the weather on Eternity's worst day? And where was that Son of God during the fatal second: pausing before a mirror in an anteroom, or in the Supreme Presence Itself, in the middle of an awful crescendo of praise, or again, withdrawn apart, regarding pensively the unspeakable beauties of the heavenly landscape?

The divinest of books says nothing. Of the primary crises of the soul no history is ever written. Yon citizen crossing the street while the policeman holds up the traffic like the Red Sea: he leaves one curb an honest man; but, ah, quickly, Constable, handcuffs out! Roll on, you heavy lorries! He is Pharaoh! Mercifully exterminate this pest! Too late, the warning cannot be given. It's done, the poison administered, the soul infected. The other curb is reached and our John Bull, honest-seeming, unsuspected, is free to walk away, within a few years to involve widows in financial ruin or a party of school children in some frightful accident.

So, on this inconceivably more catastrophic occasion, no door banged, no dog barked. There was no alarm of any kind. But consider its importance! No judge's sentence had yet been passed. Basedow's Disease had not occurred. Love. Joy. Peace. God. No words but these. No population but angels. And after . . . the whole lexicon of sin: the sullen proletariat of hell!

What, then, of the central figure in the tragedy: First among the Sons of God? Power? No Caliph or Mikado had one grain of it. Beauty? Alcibiades beside him were extraordinarily plain. Wits? Einstein were a stammerer. But for him it was not enough. For him, nothing was enough, but the unique majority of God. That or nothing! That or (ah, had he reckoned with the dread alternative!) unqualified ruin. Alas, for us he raised the question; but the answer was to lie with another!

O, even then, when the first thought tempted, was all irrevocably lost? Was there not still time, wonderful creature, to cast it from you with a phew of disgust? It doesn't matter now. Altered for ever and for the worse, he went out to corrupt others, to form his notorious and infamous societies. Gone for ever was the frank handshake, the obvious look, the direct and simple speech. The Golden Age was definitely over. Language had become symbolic, gesture a code of signals. The arrangement of books on a table conveyed a shame-faced message: flowers in a vase expressed some unsavoury *double entendre*. Personalities acquired a new and sinister significance, lost all but that. For or against: On this side of the ledger or on that. Gabriel and Michael: Out of the question. What glorious praise! Demagorgan: Safe. What a shameful comment! Abdiel and Azazael: Perhaps. Oh, beware, you unsuspecting pair! This is a terrible examination, decisive of your everlasting career. This is your only chance. There are but two colours for you to choose, the whitest white or the blackest black; salvation or damnation at one hundred per cent. Azazael chooses. What? The Black.

Miserable, unlucky he! He's failed. Now, Abdiel! You hesitate? Quick, man, the White! Bravissimo, he passes! Baffled, they slink away to make their preparations. Too late for diplomacy or apologetic telegrams. It is war.

On the details of that appalling combat, History is mercifully silent. To the vanquished, unable to consider such reminiscences without a shudder, the subject is tabu: And the victors, to whom all boasting is by nature abhorrent, have been content to leave the matter in a decent obscurity. Remember, they were divine, and therefore omniscient, omnipotent. No new-fangled auxiliary arms, the value of which is realised only by the few enthusiastic subalterns, no depth-charges or detectors, no camouflage, no poison-gas which in times of peace even generals do not see how they could bring themselves to use, no technique of deployment or barrage can have been unknown to them. It was conflict on an astronomical scale and with the gloves off. Here were no Quakers, strikers or International Red Cross, no questions of colonies or reparations. Where all were committed absolutely, there could be no ironic misgivings.

Every schoolboy knows the result. To the rebels it was destruction. The reservoirs of the Divine Wrath were inexhaustible. Nothing was signed. There was no one left to discharge so unnecessary an office. Into the fosse of Hell they fell like water. Hurrah! Hurrah! Hurrah!

Yet, my friends, you know and I know, don't we, that the events I have just narrated were not the last. Would God they had been! The scene of operations was transferred to another front, to us. Impotent to attack Him directly, the defeated sought to strike at God through His creatures, to wound where it was most tender, His artist's love. And, to our shame, they succeeded. The world became an everlasting invalid. Of course, God could have dismissed us with a snap of His fingers. One little stellar collision and . . . no more trouble for him. Why not? All reason was for it. It would have been quite cricket. But God is no eugenist. There was no talk of sterilisation, euthanasia. Only the treatment of a very merciful and loving physician. He set over us a kindly strictness, appointed His authorities, severe but just, a kind of martial law. He gave them power to govern in His name and access to His presence in their prayers, to make their reports and ask for help and guidance, that through them the people might learn His primary will.

And so, today, we are here for a very good reason. His enemies have launched another offensive, on the grandest

scale, perhaps, that this poor planet of ours has ever witnessed. As on the first awful occasion in Eden, so now:
under the same deluding banner of Freedom. For their technique of propaganda has never varied; it has been far too
successful for them to need to change it, to suggest that it
is in the human interest to destroy God. In silk-clad China
or the naked archipelagos, in the Bermudas or Brighton, in
the stone hamlet among the beechwoods or the steel flats of
the metropolis, that three-syllable whisper: "You are God,"
has been, is and, alas, will be sufficient to convert in an instant the chapped-handed but loyal ploughboy, the patient
sufferer from incurable disease, the tired economical student
or the beautiful juvenile mama into a very spiteful maniac
indeed, into whose hands modern science has placed an all-
too-efficient axe.

I should like just to try and imagine for one moment
what the world would be like if this lunacy with its grim
fanatic theories were to spread over the civilised globe. I
tell you there would exist a tyranny compared with which a
termite colony would seem dangerously lax. No family love.
Sons would inform against fathers, cheerfully send them to
the execution cellars. Mothers send their daughters to the
mines. No romance. Even the peasant must beget that standard child under laboratory conditions. Motherhood would
be by licence. Truth and Beauty would be proscribed as dangerously obstructive. To be beautiful would be treason
against the State, Thought a sabotage deadly to the thinker.
No books, no art, no music. A year of this, I say, and even
the grass would cease to grow, flowers would not risk appearance, heifers would not dare to calve.

So you see our job. To those to whom danger in God's
cause makes exclaim, like a schoolboy comforted with an
ice: "How lush!" this is a lucky day. God has given them
extraordinary privileges, but if there be any doubters, cow-
ards wavering like to cowl on an oast-house, to these I say:
"Go out of that door before it is too late!" Only those whose
decisions are swift as the sirocco, senses keen as the finest
mirror galvanometer, will constant as the standard inch and
of a chemical purity need apply. And to these I say: "Remember, God is behind you: Nelson, Henry the Fifth,
Shackleton, Julius Caesar." As for the enemy, those rats!
they shall skedaddle like a brook. Nature herself is on our
side. Their boasts are vain. You cannot threaten a thunder-
storm with a revolver. They shall be trapped by the stalks
of flowers. Sheep shall chase them away. Useless for them to

imitate natural objects: a boulder or a tree. Even the spade-handed moles shall declare their folly!

But mind, God first! To God the glory and let Him reward! God is no summer tourist. We're more than scenery to Him. He has a farmer's eye for ergot and tares. Oh delight higher than Everest and deeper than the Challenger Gulf! His commodores come into His council and His lieutenants know His love. Lord, I confess! I confess! I am all too weak and utterly unworthy. There is no other want. All actions and diversions of the people, their greyhound races, their football competitions, their clumsy acts of love, what are they but the pitiful, maimed expression of that entire passion, the positive tropism of the soul to God?

Oh Father, I am praising Thee, I have always praised Thee, I shall always praise Thee! Listen to the wooden sabots of Thy eager child running to Thy arms! Admit him to the fairs of that blessed country where Thy saints move happily about their neat, clean houses under the blue sky! O windmills, O cocks, O clouds and ponds! Mother is waving from the tiny door! The quilt is turned down in my beautiful blue and gold room! Father, I thank Thee in advance! Everything has been grand! I am coming home!

(*At the end of the sermon, the* VICAR *collapses like a wet rag into his chair and feebly mops his face with a handkerchief. There is a moment's silence: then a flourish of bugles*)

THE BOY IN COMMAND OF THE LADS OF PRESSAN
Lads! Atten-shun! Eyes . . . right!
(*The* GENERAL *and* MRS. HOTHAM *come down from the platform. The* GENERAL *is in uniform with rows of medals. His wife wears a uniform jacket and a hat with an immense white plume. They begin to inspect the Lads. Fife and drum music*)

MILDRED LUCE (*suddenly appearing from the crowd of villagers, and addressing the Lads*) I hope you know why you're really here? The Vicar daren't tell you! The General daren't tell you either! But I dare! Wave your dummy rifles about! It's only play now. But soon they'll give you real rifles. You'll learn to shoot. You'll learn to kill whoever they tell you to. And you'll be trained to let yourselves be killed, too. I thought I'd just tell you. It isn't that I care. I'm glad! What does it matter to me if you're all murdered? My sons were murdered, and they were bigger and stronger and handsomer than you'll ever be, any of you! So what do I care!

(*This speech has made the most painful impression on all present.* MRS. HOTHAM *hurriedly leads* MILDRED *off into the background and returns without her. People begin talking in undertones. The* GENERAL *abruptly cuts short the review, salutes and reascends the platform. As people still continue to whisper, he clears his throat angrily and rings a little handbell for silence*)

GENERAL   Hrrmm! Before, er, passing on to the, er, next stage in the proceedings, I should like to say how very favourably Mrs. Hotham and myself have been impresed by the excellent turn-out this afternoon.

The Lads of Pressan have made a first-rate beginning, and I hope that their end will be equally satisfactory . . . hrrmm! That is, er, I should say, I hope that they will go on as they have begun.

And now I come to an important announcement. I suppose that, by this time, it's a more or less open secret that our Patroness, Miss Iris Crewe, is engaged to be married to that well-known munitions manufacturer, hrrmm, I should say: that well-known and popular patriot and sportsman, Mr. Rudolf Trunnion-James. I'm sure we all wish her the very best of good fortune . . . hrrmm! of happiness.

Miss Crewe now authorises me to tell you that, after her marriage, she intends to present the Honeypot Hall Estate to the Lads of Pressan, as barracks, parade-ground and playing-fields. . . . Three cheers for our benefactress: Miss Iris Crewe!

(*The villagers give three cheers*)

ALAN (*from the auditorium*)   Here! I say!

GENERAL (*evidently fearing another interruption, tries to ignore* ALAN)   Miss Crewe's marriage has been fixed for the first day of next month, and I'm sure we all. . . .

ALAN   Shame!

THE GENERAL (*ringing his bell, continues*)   And I'm sure we all hope. . . .

ALAN   Stop! You've got to listen to me!

GENERAL   Confound it, sir. Can't you hear me speaking? Who the devil are you?

ALAN   Alan Norman.

(*Sensation.* ALAN *gets up from his place in the auditorium and comes on to the stage*)

ALAN   Iris, what does this mean?

IRIS (*unpleasantly surprised*)   Alan! Why have you come back?

ALAN   Because I've found Francis. (*Calling down to* FRANCIS) Francis, come up here!
(*Huge sensation.* FRANCIS *comes up on to the stage*)

IRIS   Oh, dear! I feel so ill!
(*She sways slightly in her chair and is supported by* MRS. HOTHAM, *who regards* FRANCIS *with unconcealed disapproval*)

VICAR AND GENERAL (*together: equally dismayed*)   Sir Francis! Upon my soul!

FRANCIS   Joy seems to have been too much for my dear sister's delicate constitution. . . . Hullo, General: fight back those unmanly tears! Vicar, you needn't kiss me if you don't want to. (*Looking round*) Isn't *anybody* pleased to see me?

LITTLE GIRL (*in crowd*)   Oh, I'm awfully glad you're back: Dear old Doggy!

FRANCIS   Thank you for those kind words.
(*Shakes hands with her*)
(*Everybody now becomes aware of the dog's skin which* FRANCIS *is wearing. There are murmurs of:*)
Just fancy! The Dog! He was the dog! *etc. etc.*

FRANCIS   Yes, ladies and gentlemen. The little girl is right. I am, or rather was, the Dog! (*Looking round at them*) You know, I've often pictured to myself this very moment: My return. In fact, during my canine days, it was one of my greatest pleasures. Of course, I imagined a very dramatic appearance: tearing off my disguise and denouncing you all in the kind of language to which the Vicar has just so generously treated us. But the really fascinating problem was to decide *when* to appear, and I kept putting it off. Of course, I thought, it must be just at a time when you were all cursing me and wishing I was dead. But though in private you said things about me which made my ears tingle (perhaps it did me good, too), in public you were very discreet. It was always, "poor Sir Francis," "good Sir Francis," "our wonderful lost boy squire." And now here you all are, looking extremely uncomfortable, as well you may, considering that you know I've had a dog's-eye view of you for the last ten years.
Directly after that historic row with my father (I forget exactly what it was about; I think it was the key of the gun-

room), I went upstairs to have a hot bath, feeling very injured of course, meditating suicide, running away to sea, being brought back to die of consumption, etc. And it was in the bathroom that suddenly I had the brilliant fatal idea. An hour later, my life as a dog had begun.

At first I only intended to keep my new shape for a week or two. I even doubted if I could hold out as long as that, but I had begun to keep a diary, and that helped me over the difficult period. After the first six months I didn't really want to come back. You see, I had begun to regard you in a new light. I was fascinated and horrified by you all. I thought such obscene, cruel, hypocritical, mean, vulgar creatures had never existed before in the history of the planet, and that it was my office and doom to record it. As a dog, I learnt with what a mixture of fear, bullying, and condescending kindness you treat those whom you consider your inferiors, but on whom you are dependent for your pleasures. It's an awful shock to start seeing people from underneath. My diary was my greatest friend. I worked away at it, like a scientist, polishing, punctuating, searching for the exact epithet, devoting months and even years to each one of you, noting every gesture, every intonation. I even managed to take photographs to illustrate my records, and very remarkable some of them are.

And then, slowly, the horror and the pseudoscientific interest began to wear off, too. I was growing older. I began to feel that I had been foolishly wasting my time. Hadn't it all been just a romantic escape, I asked myself? Wasn't it Life itself I was afraid of, hiding in my dog-skin? I think that, soon, I should have gone away anyhow. But, as it happened, Alan Norman was chosen. I'd always liked him and so I took the opportunity of leaving you when I did.

Don't be alarmed, I haven't come back to claim my lawful rights. Iris, you can keep Honeypot Hall and do what you like with it. I never meant to return at all. Anyhow, it wasn't necessary: you are all just as I imagined you would be. Since I've been away from you, I've come to understand you better. I don't hate you any more. I see how you fit into the whole scheme. You are significant, but not in the way I used to imagine. You are units in an immense army: most of you will die without ever knowing what your leaders are really fighting for or even that you are fighting at all. Well, I am going to be a unit in the army of the other side: but the battlefield is so huge that it's practically certain you will never see me again. We are all of us com-

pletely unimportant, so it would be very silly to start quar-
relling, wouldn't it? Goodbye.
(*He turns to go*)

ALAN   Francis! I'm coming with you!

FRANCIS   I'm glad.

IRIS   Alan!

ALAN   I know who my friends are . . . and when I'm not
wanted.

GENERAL   This is monstrous!

CURATE   Alan, I just want to say. . . .
(*He hesitates*)

ALAN   Come with us, too!

VICAR   You're lost if you do!
(*The* CURATE *hesitates between them, in great distress*)

CURATE   Christ crucified
                 Be at my side,
                 Confirm my mind
                 That it be kind
                 To those who assert and hurt
                 On either side!

                 I must go away,
                 I must go to pray
                 To One who is greater.

GENERAL   Greater than who?

CURATE   Greater than you.
(*He goes out*)

A YOUNG MAN   Francis, I'll come!
(*He crosses the stage to* FRANCIS' *side*)

A BOY FROM THE RANKS OF THE LADS OF PRESSAN
Let me come too, Francis!

FRANCIS   We're not going on a treasure-hunt, you know, or
looking for pirates.

BOY   I don't care. I want to help.

FRANCIS   All right. (*The* BOY *crosses stage*) Any more?
(*Three other villagers silently join the group*)

VICAR   If anyone else thinks of joining this mistaken young
man, I can only warn them that I shall make it my business

to see that never, at any future time, shall he or she receive employment in Pressan again.

FRANCIS (*to his followers*)   You hear what the Vicar says? Hadn't you better go back? (*Nobody moves*) Come on, then, let's be moving.
(FRANCIS, ALAN *and their five companions come down from the stage and go out through the audience*)

MRS. HOTHAM
Reginald! Can't you say something to make them feel ashamed of themselves?

GENERAL (*shouting after them*)   You're traitors to Pressan!

FRANCIS (*turning at the auditorium exit, shouts back*)   Traitors to *your* Pressan, General: not to ours!
(*He goes out, followed by the others*)
(*On the stage, everybody is talking*)

GENERAL   That young man's a disgrace to his class and his family!

IRIS (*weeping*)   Oh dear, I've never been so insulted in all my life!

MRS. HOTHAM   One can only be thankful that his poor Father isn't alive to see it!

VICAR (*burying his face in his hands*)   What a fiasco! What a scandal for Pressan! It was like a nightmare! I simply can't believe it has happened!

1ST JOURNALIST (*briskly coming forward*)   You're quite right, sir! It hasn't happened!

ALL   Hasn't happened? Whatever does he mean? We saw it, it must have happened!

2ND J.   I entirely agree with my colleague. Dozens of things occur every day, curious, embarrassing, shocking incidents: but how few of them happen! The Press disregards them: therefore they cannot have taken place! The Press is an Artist: It has a certain picture to paint. Whatever fails to harmonise with that picture, it discards; regretfully perhaps, but firmly.

1ST J.   The Press has no use for the incident you believe yourselves to have just witnessed. It has no place in our scale of values. Long-lost Baronets do not disguise themselves as dogs; or at any rate, only for erotic reasons. The behaviour of Sir Francis Crewe falls into no artistic category which we recognise: therefore it cannot be represented in our picture of the day's events.

2ND J.   And since all events are recorded by the Press, what the Press does not record cannot be an event.

1ST J.   But you, sir, and you, General, and you, Madam, you belong to our picture: These lads here, these flags, this charming old-world garden, they compose admirably. Allow me. Thank you. If you'll be so kind.
(*Talking very fast, they erect their cameras and manœuvre the somewhat bewildered* GENERAL, VICAR *and ladies into a compact group, ready to be photographed*)

2ND J.   All ready, please.
(*There is a puff of vapour and a flash so blinding that all four cover their faces with their hands. But only for an instant. Then they recover their ceremonial poses. And now, all are masked: The* GENERAL *as a Bull, the* VICAR *as a Goat,* IRIS *as a Cat and* MRS. HOTHAM *as a Turkey. They stand thus for some moments in tableau. Loud martial music. The curtain falls quickly and rises again at once. Now all the villagers wear various animal masks. The* GENERAL *is addressing them, but only a bellowing is audible. His hearers respond with various animal noises, barking, mewing, quacking, grunting, or squeaking, according to their characters. Gestures and cries become more incoherent, bestial and fantastic, until at last all are drowned in deafening military chords. The* JOURNALISTS *leave the stage through the auditorium, chatting*)

CURTAIN

Epilogue

SEMI-CHORUS I   Love, loath to enter
The suffering winter
Still willing to rejoice
With the unbroken voice
At the precocious charm
Blithe in the dream
Afraid to wake, afraid
To doubt one term

Of summer's perfect fraud,
Enter and suffer
Within the quarrel
Be most at home,
Among the sterile prove
Your vigours, love.

SEMI-CHORUS II

Mourn not for these; these are ghosts who chose their pain,
Mourn rather for yourselves; and your inability to make up
    your minds
Whose hours of self-hatred and contempt were all your maj-
    esty and crisis,
Choose therefore that you may recover: both your charity
    and your place
Determining not this that we have lately witnessed: but an-
    other country
Where grace may grow outward and be given praise
Beauty and virtue be vivid there.

SEMI-CHORUS I

Where time flows on as chalk stream clear
And lovers by themselves forgiven
The whole dream genuine, the charm mature
Walk in the great and general light
In their delight a part of heaven
Its furniture and choir.

CHORUS

To each his need: from each his power.

The Ascent of F6

A Tragedy in Two Acts

TO JOHN BICKNELL AUDEN

Ghosts whom Honour never paid,
In the foolish battle made,
Wandering through the stricken grove
Pluck the bitter herb of Love.

Characters
in the order of their appearance

Michael Forsyth Ransom

Sir James Ransom
(*His twin brother*)

Lady Isabel Welwyn

General Dellaby-Couch

Lord Stagmantle

David Gunn

Ian Shawcross

Edward Lamp

Doctor Thomas Williams

Mrs. Ransom
(*Mother of Michael and James*)

The Abbot

Mr. A.

Mrs. A.

Announcer

Blavek

Monks

Act One

Scene 1

(*The Summit of the Pillar Rock, above Wastdale. Late afternoon.* MICHAEL RANSOM *is seated, reading a pocket volume of Dante*)

RANSOM (*reads*)   "O brothers!" I said, "who through a hundred thousand dangers have reached the West, deny not, to this brief vigil of your senses that remains, experience of the unpeopled world behind the Sun. Consider your origin: ye were not formed to live like brutes, but to follow virtue and knowledge." (*Putting down the book*) Virtue and knowledge! One can picture Ulysses' audience: a crook speaking to crooks. Seedy adventurers, of whose expensive education nothing remained but a few grammatical tags and certain gestures of the head; refugees from the consequences of vice or eccentric and conceited opinions; natural murderers whom a peaceful winter had reduced to palsied wrecks; the ugly and cowardly who foresaw in a virgin land an era of unlimited and effortless indulgence; teachers without pupils, tormentors without victims, parasites without hosts, lunatic missionaries, orphans.

And glad they must have been to believe it, during the long uneventful voyage westward: yes, even up to the very end, when the last deceptions were choked from each in turn by the strangling Atlantic. Who was Dante—to whom the Universe was peopled only by his aristocratic Italian acquaintances and a few classical literary characters, the fruit of an exile's reading—who was Dante, to speak of Virtue and Knowledge? It was not Virtue those lips, which involuntary privation had made so bitter, could pray for; it was not Knowledge; it was Power. Power to exact for every snub, every headache, every unfallen beauty, an absolute revenge; with a stroke of the pen to make a neighbour's vine-yard a lake of fire and to create in his private desert the austere music of the angels or the happy extravagance of a fair. Friends whom the world honours shall lament their eternal losses in the profoundest of crevasses, while he on the green mountains converses gently with his unapproach-able love.

Virtue. Knowledge. We have heard these words before; and we shall hear them again—during the nursery luncheon, on the prize-giving afternoon, in the quack advertisement, at the conference of generals or industrial captains: justify-ing every baseness and excusing every failure, comforting the stilted schoolboy lives, charming the wax-like and ba-roque, inflaming the obstinate and the odd and all those hungry and cheerful persons whom the holiday now dis-charges into these lake-filled valleys radiating from the rocky hub on which I sit.

Beyond the Isle of Man, behind the towers of Peel Castle, the sun slides now towards the creasing sea; and it is into a Wastwater utterly in shadow that the screes now make their unhalting plunge. Along the lake shores lovers pace, each wrapped in a disturbing and estranging vision. In the white house among the pines coffee will be drunk, there will be talk of art at the week-end. Under I cannot tell how many of these green slate roofs, the stupid peasants are making their stupid children.

Nevertheless, let me receive such vigour as the impassive embraces of this sullen rock afford, from which no mastery can elicit a gratifying response, nor defeat sighs capable of despairing misinterpretation. Here is no knowledge, no com-munication, no possession; nothing that a bishop could justify, a stockbroker purchase or an elderly scientist devote years to explaining—only the voluntary homage paid by the living to the unqualified and dangerous dead. Let me pay it, then; pay it now, before I descend to the valley and all its varieties of desperation: the calculations of shop-keepers under the gas-flares and the destructive idleness of the soldier; the governess in the dead of night giving the Universe nought for behaviour and the abandonment of the prophet to the merciless curiosity of a demon; the plotting of diseases to establish an epoch of international justice and the struggle of beauty to master and transform the most recalcitrant features; the web of guilt that prisons every upright person and all those thousands of thoughtless jailers from whom Life pants to be delivered—myself not least;

all swept and driven by the possessive incompetent fury and
the disbelief. O, happy the foetus that miscarries and the
frozen idiot that cannot cry "Mama"! Happy those run over
in the street today or drowned at sea, or sure of death to-
morrow from incurable diseases! They cannot be made a
party to the general fiasco. For of that growth which in
maturity had seemed eternal it is now no tint of thought
or feeling that has tarnished, but the great ordered flower
itself is withering; its life-blood dwindled to an unimportant
trickle, stands under heaven now a fright and ruin, only to
crows and larvae a gracious refuge. . . .

VOICE OF SHAWCROSS (*from below*)   Where are you, M. F.?

VOICE OF GUNN   When you've finished saying your prayers,
we should like to go down!

VOICE OF SHAWCROSS   It'll be dark soon, if we don't make
a start.

RANSOM (*shouting back*)   All right! I'm coming!
(*He begins to descend as the* CURTAIN *falls*)

(*The Stage-Box, right, is illuminated.* MRS. A. *is discovered
cooking*)

MRS. A.   Evening. A slick and unctuous Time
Has sold us yet another shop-soiled day,
Patently rusty, not even in a gaudy box.
I have dusted the six small rooms:
The parlour, once the magnificent image of my free-
dom,
And the bedroom, which once held for me
The mysterious languors of Egypt and the terrifying
Indias.
The delivery-vans have paid their brief impersonal
visits.
I have eaten a scrappy lunch from a plate on my
knee.
I have spoken with acquaintances in the Stores;
Under our treble gossip heard the menacing throb
of our hearts
As I hear them now, as all of us hear them,

Standing at our stoves in these villas, expecting our
    husbands:
The drums of an enormous and routed army,
Throbbing raggedly, fitfully, scatteredly, madly.
We are lost. We are lost.

(*Enter* MR. A. *from work*)

MR. A.   Has anything happened?

MRS. A.   What should happen?
The cat has died at Ivy Dene,
The Crowthers' pimply son has passed Matric,
St. Neots has put up light blue curtains,
Frankie is walking out with Winnie
And George loves himself. What should happen?
Nothing that matters will ever happen.

MR. A.   No, nothing that matters will ever happen;
Nothing you'd want to put in a book;
Nothing to tell to impress your friends—
The old old story that never ends:
The eight o'clock train, the customary place,
Holding the paper in front of your face,
The public stairs, the glass swing-door,
The peg for your hat, the linoleum floor,
The office stool and the office jokes
And the fear in your ribs that slyly pokes:
Are they satisfied with you?
Nothing interesting to do,
Nothing interesting to say,
Nothing remarkable in any way;
Then the journey home again
In the hot suburban train
To the tawdry new estate,
Crumpled, grubby, dazed and late:
Home to supper and to bed.
Shall we be like this when we are dead?

MRS. A.   It's time for the news, John. Turn on the wireless.

MR. A.   I'm sick of the news. All you can hear
Is politics, politics everywhere:
Talk in Westminster, talk at Geneva, talk in the
    lobbies and talk on the throne;
Talk about treaties, talk about honour, mad dogs
    quarrelling over a bone.
What have they ever done, I ask you? What are
    they ever likely to do

To make life easier, make life happier? What have
they done for me or for you?

MRS. A.   Smiling at all the photographers, smoking, walking
in top hats down by the lake,
Treating the people as if they were pigeons, giving
the crumbs and keeping the cake.
When will they notice us? When will they flatter us?
When will they help us? When there's a war!
Then they will ask for our children and kill them;
sympathise deeply and ask for some more.

MR. A.   Night after night we have listened to the ignoble
news.

MRS. A.   We have heard
The glib justification of the sorry act.

MR. A.   The frantic washing of the grimy fact.

MRS. A.   But nothing to bring a smile to the face.

MR. A.   Nothing to make us proud of our race.

MRS. A.   Nothing we should have been glad to have done
In a dream, or would wish for an only son.

MR. A.   Nothing to take us out of ourselves,
Out of the oppression of this city,
This abstract civic space imposed upon the fields,
Destroying that tie with the nearest which in Nature
rules.

MRS. A.   Where we are unable to lose sight of the fruits of
our extraordinary industry.

MR. A.   And everything is emphatically provided:
The Dial Exchange and the voice of the lift.
We must accept them all and there is no one to
thank.

MRS. A.   Give us something to be thankful for.

MR. A.   Give it quickly.
I have read "Too Late" in the hands of the office
clock.

MRS. A.   I have received singular warnings:
In the eyes of the beggar I have experienced the
earthquake and the simoom.

MR. A.   Sitting in the crowded restaurant, I have overheard
the confabulations of weasels.

MRS. A.   Give us something to live for. We have waited too
     long.

(*The Stage-Box is darkened*)

Scene II

(SIR JAMES RANSOM'S *room at the Colonial Office. On the
wall, at the back of the stage, hangs a large boldly-printed map
showing British Sudoland and Ostnian Sudoland, coloured
respectively pink and blue. The frontier between the two colonies is formed by a chain of mountains: one peak, prominently
marked F 6, is ringed with a red circle to emphasise its importance. At a table covered with papers, maps and books of
reference are seated, from L. to R.* LORD STAGMANTLE, SIR
JAMES RANSOM, GENERAL DELLABY-COUCH *and* LADY ISABEL
WELWYN. *As the curtain rises,* JAMES *lays down a document
from which he has been reading aloud to the others*)

JAMES   That, briefly, is the position. I think you'll agree with
     me that it is deplorable.

ISABEL   But surely, surely the report exaggerates? My poor
     darling Sudoland—it's still like home to me, you know!
     No, I simply can't believe it!

JAMES   We all appreciate your feelings, Lady Isabel. They
     are most natural. Unfortunately I have reason to believe
     that this report, so far from exaggerating, may even under-
     estimate the gravity of the situation. . . . From other
     sources—not official, it is true, but as a rule absolutely re-
     liable—we hear that the whole southern province is in a
     state of uproar. Government stores have been burnt, British
     officers have been attacked. In a few hill stations, the
     women of the European settlements have been grossly in-
     sulted——

ISABEL   The cowardly fiends! How they can *dare!* In my
     father's time——

GENERAL   In your father's time, Lady Isabel, a British Gov-
     ernor was required to rule, not to coddle a native population
     according to the sentimental notions of a gang of home-bred
     politicians. The Sudoese hillman has not changed since your
     father's day: take him for what he is, he's a fine fellow.
     He's a man and he expects to be ruled by men. He under-

stands strength and he respects it. He despises weakness and he takes advantage of it. Show him the business end of a machine-gun and he'll——

JAMES (*acidly*)   I think, General, you can hardly complain that the Government of which I am a member shows any lack of respect for your great practical experience in administration. Otherwise you would not have been invited to attend this conference to-day. But I should like to suggest that, in your wholesale condemnation of politicians, you are apt to forget that we are only the servants of the public. Public opinion has changed greatly, during the last twenty years, with regard to the native populations of the Empire. There have been unfortunate incidents which unscrupulous party agitators have not hesitated to misrepresent. . . . To take your own case, that most regrettable *contretemps* at Bolo-Bolo. . . .

ISABEL   Really, Sir James, is it necessary, at a time like this, to stoop to personalities?

JAMES (*smoothly*)   My dear Lady Isabel, I'm sure I had no intention of hurting the General's feelings. General, please accept my apologies. I only wished to remind you—not, alas, that any of us need reminding—how grossly a valued public servant can be maligned in the performance of a painful duty by the venom of the popular press——

STAGMANTLE (*beginning to laugh wheezily*)   British General Butchers Unarmed Mob! Children Massacred in Mothers' Arms! Murder Stains the Jack!

JAMES (*hastily*)   Yes, yes. . . . The nauseating clichés of gutter socialism——

STAGMANTLE   Socialism my foot! Why, that's out of the *Evening Moon!* Splashed it all over the front page—nearly doubled our sales, that week! No offence, General. We were out to smash the Labour Government, you know: and, by God, we did! Your little stunt came in handy: any stick's good enough to beat a dog with, you know! Ha, ha, ha!

ISABEL   Of all the utterly low and contemptible things I ever heard . . .

JAMES (*hastily intervening*)   As Lord Stagmantle quite rightly observes, the tactical problems raised by a great democratic electorate are exceedingly complex. One must try to see things in perspective. . . . I'm sure nobody doubts Lord Stagmantle's loyalty in this present crisis. Had it not been for his assistance in presenting the events of the last month to the public in their true proportions——

STAGMANTLE   Look here, Ransom; that's just what I came to tell you today. We can't keep this up for ever, you know. *The Thunderbolt* has been featuring the Sudoland revolts now for a week or more. How much longer do you expect us to play hush-hush? It's beginning to affect our circulation already. You've got to do something, quick.

ISABEL   But surely, Lord Stagmantle, all this suppression and misrepresentation of facts is a very mistaken policy? Why can't you have more courage? Why not let the public judge for itself? I should have thought that the truth——

STAGMANTLE   The truth, Lady Isabel, is that the natives of British Sudoland would like us to go to hell—pardon my language—and stay there. The truth is that we've got ten millions invested in the country and we don't intend to budge—not if we have to shoot every nigger from one end of the land to the other. The truth is that we're under-garrisoned and under-policed and that we're in a blue funk that the Ostnians will come over the frontier and drive us into the sea. Already, they've spent thousands on propaganda among our natives, promising reforms which neither they nor we nor any other colonial power could ever carry out. This revolt is the result. . . . There's the truth for you: and you want me to tell that to the public! What do you take me for—a bolshevik?

JAMES   Lord Stagmantle is perfectly right: though, with his characteristic flair for essentials, he oversimplifies the situation, perhaps, a little. . . . He asks me to do something. I shall not disappoint him. I did not call this meeting merely in order to alarm you. His Majesty's Government has a plan. (*He rises and points dramatically to the map on the wall, indicating F 6*) The key to the problem lies there!

ISABEL   Why, but that's the Haunted Mountain! I used to be able to see it from my bedroom window at the Residency, when the weather was clear. . . . Let me think, now, what did the natives call it?

JAMES   The mountain has, I understand, many local names; most of them unpronounceable. The survey refers to it simply as F 6.

STAGMANTLE   A haunted mountain, eh? What's the story in it?

JAMES   Merely that the mountain is said to be haunted by a
guardian demon. For this reason, no native will set foot
upon it. As you will notice, it stands exactly on the frontier
line. Both Ostnia and ourselves claim it; but, up to the
present, no European has ever visited the district at all.

ISABEL   I remember, when I was a little girl, being afraid
that the demon would come and carry me away with him
to the top! Aren't children absurd?

GENERAL   May I ask if we came here this morning to discuss
fairy-tales?

JAMES   A fairy-tale, General, is significant according to the
number of people who believe in it. This one is credited by
several millions of natives on both sides of the frontier. . . .
Also, the legend has lately developed a sequel which may
appeal more strongly to your imagination: The natives have
begun telling each other that the white man who first
reaches the summit of F 6, will be lord over *both* the Sudo-
lands, with his descendants, for a thousand years.

STAGMANTLE   Aha, so that's their little game! The Ostnians
started this yarn, of course?

JAMES   You are very quick to follow me, Lord Stagmantle.
And perfectly correct. Yes, the Ostnian agents have been
propagating this story for the past six months. We've traced
it right down into the plains.

GENERAL   But, Ransom, you don't seriously suggest that the
Ostnians expect to gain anything by spreading this absurd
nonsense? The hillmen may believe them, I admit—the
Sudoese are credulous beggars—but, hang it all, what good
can it do Ostnia? None whatever. If you ask me, this is just
another Ostnian bluff. Bluffing's their strong suit.

JAMES   I wish I could agree with you, General. But this
morning this telegram reached us, through the Intelligence.
(*Reads*) Expedition under Blavek left Ostnia for Ostnian
Sudoland yesterday great secrecy intending attempt ascent
of F 6.

ISABEL   Monstrous!

GENERAL   The beggars are mad as coots!

STAGMANTLE   Not so mad as you may think, General. I
ought to know something about propaganda stunts: this is
one of the best I ever struck. If the Ostnians get to the top

of F 6, your natives are going to make big trouble. Whether you like it or not, you'll have to start shooting. And Ostnia will intervene, in the name of the poor oppressed subject races. They'll have world opinion on their side, into the bargain. . . . You're in a cleft stick.

ISABEL   Can't we send a cruiser to stop this expedition?

STAGMANTLE   Certainly. If you care to start a European war.

GENERAL   At any rate, these chaps will never reach the summit.

JAMES   We can't be too sure of that, I'm afraid. There's a great deal at stake.

ISABEL   You sit here calmly and say so! Oh, if only I were a man! What are you going to *do?*

JAMES   His Majesty's Government proposes to send an expedition to Sudoland without delay.

ISABEL   Oh, good! Good!

STAGMANTLE   Now you're talking!

GENERAL   Never heard such damned tomfoolery in all my life!

STAGMANTLE   I must congratulate you, Ransom. You're on to a big thing—a big thing for all of us! The *Evening Moon* will subscribe two thousand to the funds of the expedition . . .

JAMES   (*shaking hands with him*)   I knew we could rely on your public spirit, Lord Stagmantle!

STAGMANTLE   . . . provided, of course, that we get the exclusive rights—pictures, film, lecture-tours, story. We can discuss details later. . . .

JAMES   (*rather taken aback*)   Er, yes, quite so, of course——

ISABEL   And now, there's not a moment to be lost! We must think quickly: who are you going to send? How will you find the right man to lead them?

JAMES   I am happy to say that I have found him already.

ISABEL   You've found him! Oh, Sir James, I think you're wonderful! Who is he?

JAMES   My brother.

ISABEL   You have a brother! And we never even knew!

JAMES   My brother Michael is considered, by competent experts, to be one of the best climbers in this country.

ISABEL   How I should adore to meet him—the man who can save Sudoland!

JAMES   We'll go to him at once. My car is waiting. (*To* GENERAL *and* STAGMANTLE) You'll come with us, I hope?

GENERAL   I refuse to be a party to this wild goose chase. When you have ceased to occupy yourselves with demons and need some serious advice, you will find me at my club. Good morning.

ISABEL   Oh, General!
(*The* GENERAL, *taking no notice, goes out*)

STAGMANTLE   Never mind him, Lady Isabel. . . . A remarkable old gentleman, but conservative: no vision. He'll come round to the idea in time. . . . (*Rubbing his hands gleefully*) Well, Ransom, let's see this brother of yours! I'll write the interview myself! By George, what a day for the *Evening Moon!*

ISABEL   (*reprovingly*)   What a day for *England,* Lord Stagmantle!

STAGMANTLE   Oh, England—yes, quite so, of course. (*Looking up at map*) The Ascent of F 6!
(*All three of them stand regarding the map in reverent silence as the——*)

CURTAIN FALLS

(*The Stage-Boxes, left and right, are illuminated. In the right Box,* MR. A. *sits listening to the radio* ANNOUNCER, *who speaks from the Box on the left*)

ANNOUNCER   If you drink coffee for breakfast, you will be familiar with Sudoland as the name of one of the most delicious brands in the world, said by connoisseurs to be equal even to Blue Mountain and only half the price. But, unless you have a brother or a nephew there, I don't expect you know much more about this beautiful and exciting country. It is about as big as Ireland and embraces a wide variety of scenery and climate, from the moist hot river-plains in the north to the magnificent escarpment of mountains on the southern border. The natives are delightful people, of wonderful physique and very humorous and artistic. Their vil-

lages consist of mud huts and they live very simply, chiefly
on boiled bamboo shoots, which they call KHA. Most of
them are employed on the coffee estates, where they make
excellent workmen. You may have read recently, in some
of the papers, of riots in Sudoland, but from personal experience I can tell you that these stories have been grossly
exaggerated. They were confined to a very small section of
irresponsibles egged on by foreign agitators. Hospitals,
clinics and schools have done much to raise the standard
of personal hygiene and education among the Sudoese and
the vast majority are happy and contented.

(*At this point,* MRS. A. *enters the Stage-Box, right, bringing coffee*)

If ever I make enough money to retire from journalism,
it is to a small hill-station in Sudoland called Fort George
that I should like to go, to spend the evening of my days. I
have knocked about the world a good deal and seen most
of the famous views, but never have I seen anything to com-
pare with the one you get from the English Cemetery there.
From this point you see the whole mountain range which
culminates in that terrifying fang of rock and ice called so
prosaically on our maps "F 6," but in the native tongue
"Chormopuloda"—that is, the Haunted Mountain. There
are many legends about this mountain and the troll who
lives on the summit and devours all human beings who dare
approach it. No Europeans have, so far, ventured into this
region, which is barren to a degree and inhabited only by
monks who resent foreigners. These monks practise a mysterious cult which is believed to be descended from the
religion of Ancient Egypt; and there are wonderful tales
current of their mystical and psychic powers. Be that as it
may, I do not think it likely that it will be long before our
young climbers will discover a new ground for their sport,
offering more magnificent opportunities for their skill and
their love of nature, than even those afforded by the Alps
or the Himalayas. . . .

(*Exit*)

MRS. A.   It's all very well for him, he can travel.

MR. A.   Cousin Bertie's boy was there:
Poor lad, he had to come home last year:
They've reduced the staff on his coffee estate.
He said that the people and country were great.

MRS. A.   Why do you never take me abroad?

MR. A.   Darling, you know that we can't afford. . . .

MRS. A.   Afford! It's always the same excuse—
Money, money!

MR. A.   Dear, what's the use
Of talking like this?

MRS. A.   You don't really care;
If you did, we shouldn't be here.
Why don't you do something, something that pays,.
    Not be a clerk to the end of your days?
A dreary little clerk on a dreary little screw—
Can't you find something proper to do?
But you don't care, it's the same to you
Whether I live or whether I die.
I wish I were dead!

MR. A.   Mary, don't cry!
You never know, perhaps one day
Better luck will come our way:
It might be tomorrow. You wait and see.
But, whenever it happens, we'll go on the spree!
From the first-class gilt saloon of channel-steamer
    we shall peer,
While the cliffs of Dover vanish and the Calais flats
    appear,
Land there, take the fastest train, have dinner in the
    dining-car,
Through the evening rush to Paris, where the ladies'
    dresses are.
Nothing your most daring whisper prayed for in the
    night alone—
Evening frocks and shoes and jewels; you shall have
    them for your own.
Rome and Munich for the opera; Mürren for the
    winter sports;
See the relics of crusaders in the grey Dalmatian
    ports;
Climb the pyramids in Egypt; walk in Versailles'
    ordered parks;
Sail in gondolas at Venice; feed the pigeons at St.
    Mark's. . . .

MRS. A.   O, what's the use of your pretending?
As if life had a chance of mending!
There will be nothing to remember
But the fortnight in August or early September,

The boarding-house food, the boarding-house faces,
The rain-spoilt picnics in the windswept places,
The camera lost and the suspicion,
The failure in the putting-competition,
The silly performance on the pier—
And it's going to happen again next year!

MR. A.   Mary!

MRS. A.   Don't touch me! Go away! Do you hear?
(*She bursts into tears; he shrugs his shoulders and goes out, slamming the door. The Box is darkened*)

Scene III

(*Parlour of a public house in the Lake District. Shabby late Victorian furniture. A window at the back gives a view towards the fells. By the door, L. is a telephone. On the right, a cottage piano. After supper. At a large table, in the centre of the stage,* MICHAEL RANSOM *and the* DOCTOR *are playing chess. At a smaller table, L.* LAMP *is bending over a microscope. In an armchair, R.* SHAWCROSS *is writing in a notebook.* GUNN *is at the piano, strumming and singing. As he writes,* SHAWCROSS *frowns with suppressed annoyance*)

GUNN (*singing*)   The chimney sweepers
    Wash their faces and forget to wash the neck;
The lighthouse keepers
    Let the lamps go out and leave the ships to wreck;
The prosperous baker
    Leaves the rolls in hundreds in the oven to burn;
The undertaker
    Pins a small note on the coffin saying "Wait till I return,
I've got a date with Love!"
And deep-sea divers
    Cut their boots off and come bubbling to the top,
And engine-drivers
    Bring expresses in the tunnel to a stop;
The village rector
    Dashes down the side-aisle half-way through a psalm;
The sanitary inspector
    Runs off with the cover of the cesspool on his arm—
To keep his date with Love!

(*Jumps up from the piano and goes over to* SHAWCROSS)
Still sweating at that old diary?

SHAWCROSS   I was doing my best to, in spite of your filthy
row.

GUNN   So glad you enjoyed it, dearie. I'll play you something
else. (*Goes back to piano*)

RANSOM   Shut up, David. (*To* DOCTOR) Check.

GUNN   (*leaving piano and looking over* SHAWCROSS' *shoulder*)
Hullo, what's all this? (*Reads*) ". . . followed up a splendid short pitch to the north summit. Gunn, as usual . . ."

SHAWCROSS   (*snatching book*)   Leave that alone, damn you!

GUNN   (*grabs book back and reading*)   ". . . Gunn, as usual,
fooling about, completely irresponsible. I can never understand M. F.'s patience with him. . . ."
(SHAWCROSS *tries to snatch book.* GUNN *dodges round the
chair*)

SHAWCROSS   Give it here, blast your eyes!

GUNN   Ha, ha! Wouldn't you like it! Why can't you be
patient with me, like M. F.?

SHAWCROSS   You little fool! Do you want me to hurt you?

RANSOM   Give it back, David. (*To* DOCTOR) Check.

GUNN   Sorry, Ian. You're not cross with me, are you? Come
and have a drink?

SHAWCROSS   Surely you ought to know by this time that I
never drink the day before a climb.

GUNN   To hear you talk, one'd think we were a lot of monks.

SHAWCROSS   It just happens that I take climbing seriously.
You don't.

GUNN   All right. Keep your hair on. No offence. (*Strolls over
to* LAMP) Let's have a squint, Teddy. (*Looks into microscope*) What's this stuff that looks like mouldy cheese?

LAMP   If I were to tell you, you wouldn't be any the wiser.

GUNN   No, I expect I shouldn't. (*He wanders over to watch
the chess players*)

SHAWCROSS   M. F., may I take your climbing boots? I'd like
to oil them for you.

RANSOM   It's very kind of you, Ian; but I gave them to the
maid.

SHAWCROSS   I wish you wouldn't, M. F. How can you expect a girl to oil boots? I'll just do them over again, myself.

RANSOM (*smiling*)   You spoil me, Ian. One day, you'll regret it. I shall become as helpless as a baby without its nurse.

SHAWCROSS (*blushing*)   It's no trouble at all. I like to keep things decent.

GUNN (*yawning and stretching himself*)   Gosh, I'm bored! If I had a thousand pounds, I'd buy an aeroplane and try to fly across the Atlantic: if I had five hundred pounds, I'd go to Africa and shoot lions. As it is, I've got seven and elevenpence, so I suppose I'd better get drunk.
(*As he moves towards the door, the telephone rings*)

SHAWCROSS   I expect that'll be the man about the new ropes. (*Goes to telephone*) Hullo. . . . No, it's a call from London. (*To* GUNN) For you.

GUNN   Ask who it is. Wait a minute. . . . Don't, for Heaven's sake, say I'm here!

RANSOM (*To* DOCTOR)   Look out for that castle, Tom.

SHAWCROSS   Who's speaking? (*To* GUNN) It's a lady. A Mrs. da Silva.

GUNN   Gosh, that's torn it! Tell her I've gone away! Tell her I'm dead!

SHAWCROSS (*listening*)   She says she knows you're here and that it's no good saying you aren't. (*Holding out receiver to* GUNN) Here, take it! I'm not going to do your dirty work for you.

GUNN (*after making frantic signals, advances gingerly to the telephone*)   Oh, hullo, darling—how lovely to hear your voice! No, of *course* not! How *could* you think so! Well, you know, I'm terribly busy just now. I *could* get up to town this week-end, if it's really absolutely necessary. . . . No, darling, I *swear* there isn't! Listen, here comes a kiss! *Goodbye!* (*Hanging up receiver and mopping his forehead*) And now *she's* on the track again! Says her husband's going to divorce her! Oh, whatever shall I do?

SHAWCROSS   I hardly see what else you can expect, when you've got about as much self-control as a tom-cat. . . . What we do object to is the way you involve us all in your nasty little intrigues.

GUNN Everybody seems to be finding out my address. This morning, I had five more bills. . . . Oh, if only I could get right out of England for six months, they might forget about me.

RANSOM Check.

DOCTOR (*making a move*) Aha, M. F., that's got you! . . . No, it hasn't. . . . Oh, dear!

RANSOM Mate. Thank you, Tom.

DOCTOR Why do I always do something silly when I play with you? It's no good. You get me every time. (*Rising*) Oh, I'm so fat, I'm so fat!

GUNN Doc., I believe you forgot your exercises this morning!

DOCTOR As if I ever forgot them! As if I ever could forget them! (*Sighs*) Perhaps it would be better if I stopped them altogether. But I haven't the nerve.

GUNN Poor old Doc.! Come and have a drink. Whisky shrivels up your flesh.

DOCTOR Do you really think so? I've got to a stage where I can believe almost anything.
(*A knock at the door*)

ISABEL'S VOICE May we come in?

GUNN Another woman! Don't open it, for the Lord's sake! Let me hide! (*Dives under the larger table*)
(SHAWCROSS *opens the door. Enter* LADY ISABEL, *followed by* STAGMANTLE *and* SIR JAMES RANSOM)

ISABEL (*to James*) I told you they'd be in here!

RANSOM (*unpleasantly surprised*) James!

JAMES Ah, Michael, there you are! Very glad to find you at home. I thought I'd pay you a surprise visit. I've brought some friends who were anxious to meet you. . . . May I introduce my brother—Lady Isabel Welwyn, Lord Stagmantle.

RANSOM (*with a rather stiff bow*) How do you do? These are my friends—Doctor Williams, Mr. Shawcross, Mr. Lamp. . . . David, come out. . . . (GUNN *scrambles out from under the table*) Mr. Gunn.

GUNN (*politely*) How do you do?

JAMES (*to* RANSOM)   I've been telling Lady Isabel and Lord Stagmantle about your climbing exploits. They were greatly interested.

ISABEL   You know, Mr. Ransom, you're not a bit like Sir James! I should never have taken you for brothers, at all!

STAGMANTLE   It's a great pleasure to meet you, Mr. Ransom. I'm always glad to make contacts with prominent personalities, in any walk of life. Sir James tells me that you have many sidelines. You're a scholar, I believe? Well, now, that intrigues me. Scholar and man of action: an unusual mixture, eh?

JAMES   As I never fail to observe, my brother has all the brains of our family. In all humility I say it—my brother is a great man.

RANSOM (*who has listened to the above remarks with growing uneasiness, now turns on* JAMES *and blurts out*)   Why have you come here? What do you want?

JAMES (*smiling awkwardly*)   Hardly very friendly, are you, Michael? How do you know that I want anything—beyond the pleasure of seeing you again after so long?

RANSOM   How often, when we were boys, you used to come to me as you come today, with that peculiar smile on your face, half impudent, half timid! What do you want this time —my toy engine, my cricket bat, my rare West Indian stamps? Or shall I do you a favour—run that errand to the butcher's, correct your Latin verses, clean the motor-bicycle? Let's hear what it is, James: we're grown men now.

JAMES (*with a change of manner*)   You are quite right, Michael. I shall not waste words. There is no time to lose. (*Lowering his voice*) Isn't it possible for me to speak to you alone?

RANSOM   If you have no secrets from your friends, I have none from mine.

JAMES   Very well, since you wish it. . . . (*Clearing his throat*) In the name of His Majesty's Government, I have come to make you a most important proposition——

RANSOM   Which I unconditionally refuse.

JAMES (*taken aback*)   But—Michael—I haven't even told you what it is!

RANSOM   You have told me quite enough. I know your propositions, James: they are all alike. They are exceedingly convincing. They contain certain reservations. They are concerned with prestige, tactics, money and the privately pre-arranged meanings of familiar words. I will have nothing to do with any of them. Keep to your world. I will keep to mine.

JAMES   You are not being fair to me, Michael. You have never been fair to me. What I am offering you is an opportunity—the greatest of your whole life—to do something after your own heart. We want you to lead an expedition which will attempt the ascent of F 6.

RANSOM (*startled*)   F 6! What have you and your world to do with F 6?

JAMES   Ah, you see, Michael; I told you you would be intested!

RANSOM   Since boyhood, in dreams, I have seen the huge north face. On nights when I could not sleep I worked up those couloirs, crawled along the eastern arrête, planning every movement, foreseeing every hold. Through how many thousand years have those virgin buttresses been awaiting me! F 6 is my fate. . . . But not now. Not like this! No, no, no! I refuse!

JAMES   But, Michael, this is sheer caprice! I must explain: the future of England, of the Empire, may be at stake. Weighty political considerations, the Government——

RANSOM   And your own career? Be honest, James, and add the heaviest weight to the scales. . . . No, I am sorry, but F 6 is more important to me even than that. I will not go.

ISABEL   Mr. Ransom, if you lead this expedition—no matter whether you succeed or fail: and of course you *will* succeed —there is not a woman in England who will not feel proud of you—*more* than proud! I appeal to you, as an Englishwoman, in the name of all Englishwomen. You refused your brother. Can you refuse *me?*

RANSOM   I can refuse you, Lady Isabel.

ISABEL   You disappoint me, Mr. Ransom. Sir James made me hope great things of you. He was too generous. I had never expected this. I see it in your eyes. You are afraid.

RANSOM   I am afraid of a great many things, Lady Isabel. But of nothing which you in your worst nightmares could ever imagine; and of that word least of all.

STAGMANTLE Look here, Ransom; let's understand each other. I'm not going to talk a lot of blarney to you about England and Idealism. I'm a practical man. You're a practical man—of course you are! Only failures are idealists. My dear fellow, think what this climb will mean to you! Cash, and lots of it! You need cash to pursue your hobby? Of course you do! Look at it in a sensible light. (*Lowers his voice*) Between ourselves, this expedition's nothing more or less than a political racket. You know that. So do I. Well, who cares! Leave the dirty work to your brother and me: we're used to it. Forget about us. Go out to F 6 and enjoy yourself. Make climbing history. By God, I envy you! If I were twenty years younger, I swear I'd ask you to take me along!

RANSOM I like your reasons best, Lord Stagmantle. And I respect you. You talk like a man. I'd rather have you in front of me on a rope than behind me with a loudspeaker. . . . I am sorry. I know you won't understand my refusal. But I do refuse.

STAGMANTLE Is that your last word?

RANSOM It is.
(*There is a knock at the door*)

STAGMANTLE Too bad. . . . Well, Ransom, it seems we shall have to look elsewhere.

JAMES (*triumphantly*) Not yet! (*He goes to the door, opens it and speaks to someone outside*) Ah, splendid! So you got my telegram? Yes, he's here! (*Enter* MRS. RANSOM) Here is somebody who may be able to persuade you, Michael!

RANSOM (*with a cry of dismay*) Mother!

MOTHER (*advancing to* RANSOM) Michael, I am so proud——

RANSOM (*recoiling*) You too! No, it is impossible!
You come so late, it is an accident
Your shadow adds to theirs, a trick of the light.
If this was purposed——
(*In the course of the following dialogue, the light becomes entirely concentrated upon* RANSOM *and his* MOTHER. *The rest of the stage is darkened: the other figures being seen only as indistinct shapes in the background*)

MOTHER I have no purpose but to see you happy,
And do you find that so remarkable?
What mother could deny it and be honest?

I know my son the greatest climber in the world;
I know F 6 the greatest mountain in the world.
May not a mother come at once to bring
Her only gift, her love? When the news came,
I was in bed, for lately
I've not been very well. But what's a headache
When I can stand beside my son and see him
In the hour of his triumph?

RANSOM   If I have triumphed
It is not as you think. I have refused it.

MOTHER

Refused it? Why? But no—I must not question
My grown-up son. You have your reasons, and I
Shall try to trust them always.
James, I remember——

RANSOM

James! Was there no other name you could remember,
No niece or cousin? Ever since we were born
I have heard the note of preference in your voice:
And must I hear it now? When we could barely walk,
I watched him romping through the children's party;
When we were boys at school,
I saw him charm his way to every heart
And idly win the prizes.
That would not matter; we are older now
And I have found myself. But James who has
The gaping world to ogle with his speeches
Must fill the last gap in his great collection
And pot-hunt for his brother. Years ago
He stole my share of you; and must he now
Estrange me even from myself?

MOTHER   Michael,
There is a secret I have kept so long
My tongue is rusty. What you have said
I knew and I have always known. Why do you start?
You are my Michael and I know my own:
A mother has no heaven but to look.
That was your secret; there is also mine:
From the good day when both of you were born,
And I first held you both in my two arms,
James, bigger, prettier, the doctor's pride,
Responding promptly to the nurse's cluck,
And you, the tiny, serious and reserved,

I knew your natures. You never knew your father:
But I can never see James toss his head
Or laugh, or take a lady's arm, but I
Must see your father in his popular pulpit.
Everyone thought your father wonderful
And so did I, until I married him
And knew him for a shell: James is like him,
He cannot live an hour without applause.
No one can say that I have stinted it.
But you, you were to be the truly strong
Who must be kept from all that could infect
Or weaken; it was for you I steeled my love
Deliberately and hid it. Do you think that it was easy
To shut you out? I who yearned to make
My heart the cosiest nook in all the world
And warm you there for ever, so to leave you
Stark to the indifferent blizzard and the lightning?
How many nights have I not bit my pillow
As the temptation fought to pick you out of bed
And cover you with kisses? But I won.
You were to be unlike your father and your brother,
You were to have the power to stand alone;
And to withhold from loving must be all my love.
I won, I said—but was the victory real?
There was a mother crucified herself
To save her favourite son from weakness,
Unlike his twin, his brother who depended
Upon the constant praises of the little.
She saved him nothing: he must have them too
Because his brother had them. She had died
To make him free; but when the moment came
To choose the greatest action of his life
He could not do it, for his brother asked him
And he was padlocked to a brother's hatred——

RANSOM   Mother, stop!

MOTHER   Michael! You mean——?

RANSOM   Yes. Go to James and tell him that you won. And
may it give him pleasure.

MOTHER   My boy!
      (*She attempts to embrace him. He turns away*)
                    BLACK OUT
(*Music. The darkness is filled with* VOICES *of* NEWSBOYS,
screaming like cats)

Evening Special! Evening Special!
Ransom to Lead Expedition!
Famous Climber's Decision!
Evening Moon: Late Night Final!
Young English Climber's Daredevil Attempt!
The Haunted Mountain: Full Story and Pictures!
Monasteries in Sudoland: Amazing Revelations!
(*The Stage-Box on the right is illuminated.* MRS. A. *is reading a morning paper*)

MRS. A.   I read the papers; there is nothing there
But news of failure and despair:
The savage train-wreck in the dead of night,
The fire in the school, the children caught alight,
The starving actor in the oven lying,
The cashier shot in the grab-raid and left dying,
The young girl slain upon the surgeon's table,
The poison-bottle with the harmless label,
The workman fallen in the scalding vat,
The father's strained heart stopping as he sat,
The student driven crazy by his reading,
The roadside accident hopelessly bleeding,
The bankrupt quaking at the postman's knock,
The moaning murderer baited in the dock——

(*Enter* MR. A. *with evening paper*)

MR. A.   Look, Mary! Read this!
(*As they read,* VOICES *are heard from the darkness of the stage*)

VOICES   Michael Forsyth Ransom.
Eight stone six. Aged twenty-eight years.
Short and blue-eyed.
His first experiences the rectory elms and the garden quarry.
Kept a tame rook. Was privately educated,
By a Hungarian tutor.
Climbed the west buttress of Clogwyn Du'r Arddu
While still in his teens. The late Colonel Bow said:
"That boy will go far."
Visited Switzerland; in a single season
Made a new traverse on the Grandes Jorasses,
Did the Furggen Shoulder and the Green Needle of Chamonix.
Studied physiology in Vienna under Niedermeyer,
Went to the Julian Alps,
Conquered Triglav, mastered the Scarlet Crag.

Disappeared into Asia Minor, appeared in the Caucasus
On two-headed Ushba, returned to England,
In an old windmill near the mouth of the Nen
Translated Confucius during a summer.
Is unmarried. Hates dogs. Plays the viola da gamba.
Is said to be an authority on Goya.
Drinks and eats little but is fond of crystallized apri-
    cots. . . .
(*The Stage-Box on the left is illuminated.* LORD STAGMANTLE
is seen at the microphone)

STAGMANTLE   It goes without saying that the other members
of the Expedition are the finest flower of English Mountaineering; and, in hands as capable and brilliant as these,
the honour and prestige of Britain, may, I am sure, be safely
left. In this machine-ridden age, some people are tempted to
suppose that Adventure is dead; but the spirit of Man has
never refused to respond to the challenge of the unknown
and men will always be found ready to take up the gauntlet,
mindless of worldly profit, undaunted by hardship and risk,
unheeding the dull spirit which can only sneer: Cui bono?
From such pioneers, the man in the street may learn to play
his part in the great game of life, small though it may be,
with a keener zest and daring——(*Exit*)
(*Meanwhile, the* A.'s *have been cutting photographs and articles out of the paper and pinning them to the walls of the
Box*)

MR. A.   Cut out the photos and pin them to the wall,
    Cut out the map and follow the details of it all,
    Follow the progress of this mountain mission,
    Day by day let it inspire our lowly condition.

MRS. A.   Many have come to us often with their conscious
        charms,
    They stood upon platforms and madly waved their
        arms,
    At the top of their voices they promised all we lack,
    They offered us glory but they wanted it back.

MR. A.   But these are prepared to risk their lives in action
    In which the peril is their only satisfaction.
    They have not asked us to alter our lives
    Or to eat less meat or to be more kind to our wives.
(LADY ISABEL *appears at the microphone in the Stage-Box,*
L.)

ISABEL   The Englishman is reserved. He does not wear his
heart on his sleeve nor put his best goods in his shop-win-
dow. He smokes his pipe and answers in words of one
syllable. So that those who do not know him think that
he is stupid and cold. But every now and then, now in this
part of the world, now in that, something generous, something brave or beautiful, just happens. And when we start
to investigate it we shall generally find that, at the bottom
of it all, is an Englishman. I have had the privilege of meeting Mr. Ransom and his companions on this expedition personally; and I can say with absolute sincerity that never in
my life have I come away feeling so exalted, so proud that
I belonged to the same country and the same race as these
gallant men. . . . (*Exit*)

MRS. A.   They make no promise to improve our station,
        At our weakness they make no show of indignation,
        They do not offer contemptuously to lend a hand
        But their courage is something the least can under-
            stand.

MR. A.   The corner tobacconist and the booking-clerk,
        The naked miner hewing in the dark,
        The forge-hand sweating at the huge steam-hammer,
        The girl imprisoned in the tower of a stammer——

MRS. A.   The invalid, sheep-counting all the night,
        The small, the tall, the black-haired and the white
        See something each can estimate,
        They can read of these actions and know them great.
(GUNN *appears at the microphone in the Stage-Box, left*)

GUNN   I don't really know exactly what to say. We none of
us know what F 6 is going to be like. If you ask me, I
think she's probably an ugly old maid. I'm scared stiff, but
Ransom will hold our hands, I expect. . . . We shall be a
jolly party; at least, I hope so. I've been on one or two of
these expeditions and no one's murdered me yet. They say
that there's a ghost at the top; but I've made Doctor Williams promise that if we see anything he'll let me hide behind him. Well, I don't think I've got anything else to say,
so I'll tell you a limerick I've just made up:
        There was an old man of F 6
        Who had some extraordinary tricks:
        He took off——
(*An* ANNOUNCER *comes hastily into the Box, pushes* GUNN
aside and speaks into the microphone)

ANNOUNCER   We are all most grateful to Mr. Gunn for his very very interesting talk. Listeners will no doubt join us in wishing the party every success. There will now be a short interval in the programme.

(*Exit* BOTH. *Stage-Box, left, is darkened*)

MRS. A.   John, I'm so happy! Can't we do something to celebrate?

MR. A.   Let's go away for the week-end. Let's go now!

MRS. A.   But it's seven o'clock and supper's nearly ready!

MR. A.   O, bother the supper! Let it burn!

MRS. A.   Let's go away and never return;
Catch the last train to——

MR. A.   Where to?

MRS. A.   What does it matter?
Anywhere out of this rush and this clatter!
Get your toothbrush, get your pyjamas,
Fetch your razor and let us be gone,
Hurry and pack, may we never come back;
For Youth goes quickly and Age comes on!

(*They begin to put on their outdoor clothes, pack, etc.*)

MR. A.   Dover would like us, Margate would welcome us,
Hastings and Folkestone would give us a part,
Hove be excited and Brighton delighted,
Southend would take us warm to her heart.

BOTH   Moments of happiness do not come often,
Opportunity's easy to miss.
O, let us seize them, of all their joy squeeze them,
For Monday returns when none may kiss!

(*Exeunt*)

(*After the* A.'*s have departed for Hove, the stage boxes are darkened. A sudden penumbra of light on the stage shows* MRS. RANSOM *seated in a high-backed chair facing the audience*)

MRS. RANSOM (*Talking to herself in a hoarse and penetrating whisper*)   Michael . . . Michael darling, can you hear me? here, there. . . . It's all right. . . . There's nothing to be frightened about. Mother's with you. Of course she won't leave you alone, Michael, never. Wherever you are, whatever you're doing, whether you know it or not, she's near you with her love; for you belong to her always. She's with you now, at sea, on board the ship with your foolish companions, and she'll be with you on the mountain, too. . . . Of course you'll get to the top, darling. Mother will help you. She'll always help you. Wasn't she with you from the very beginning, when you were a tiny baby? Of course she was! And she'll be with you at the very end . . .

RANSOM (*voice heard, very far off, frightened*) It's the Demon, Mother!

MRS. RANSOM (*sings*)

> Michael, you shall be renowned,
> When the Demon you have drowned,
> A cathedral we will build
> When the Demon you have killed.
> When the Demon is dead,
> You shall have a lovely clean bed.
>
> You shall be mine, all mine,
> You shall have kisses like wine,
> When the wine gets into your head,
> Mother will see that you're not misled;
> A saint am I and a saint are you,
> It's perfectly, perfectly, perfectly true.

BLACK OUT

Act Two

Scene 1

(*Scene: F 6. Room in a monastery on the Great Glacier. A high, gloomy vaulted chamber with doors L. into the courtyard and R. into the interior of the building. In the back wall, arches open into a cloister, beyond which the greenish faintly glowing ice of the glacier is visible.* MICHAEL RANSOM *and* SHAWCROSS *are seated at a table in the foreground, on which stand three silver candlesticks with church candles of coloured wax.* RANSOM *and* SHAWCROSS *both have notebooks and pencils. They are checking stores*)

RANSOM   How many tins of malted milk?

SHAWCROSS   Fifty.

RANSOM   How are we off for dried figs?

SHAWCROSS   Two boxes. And three of dates and five of apricots.

RANSOM   We must remember to ask the monks for yak butter. . . . How about the petrol for the Primus?

SHAWCROSS   God, that reminds me! (*He jumps up and goes to the door L. Looks out into the courtyard*) Two porters haven't finished unloading it *yet!* (*Shouts*) Hi! Sing ko, pan no ah! Teng fang! Naga! Naga! (*Returns to table*) Lazy devils! And it'll be dark in a few minutes. . . . That's what comes of leaving things to Gunn. He treats this whole business like a picnic. (*He glances quickly at* RANSOM, *who does not, however, respond*)

RANSOM   Have we got enough soup cubes?

SHAWCROSS   Three large packets. (*Hesitates*) Look here, M. F., I've been wanting to talk to you about Gunn for a long time now. . . . You know, I hate to bother you with this sort of thing. . . . I've tried to keep you from noticing. . . .

RANSOM (*smiles*)   Have you?

SHAWCROSS   You mean you *did* see something? Well, in a way I'm glad. Because, if you hadn't, you mightn't have believed me——

RANSOM   I saw that Gunn teased the yaks and scared the porters and played tricks on Tom and Teddy, and on you too, Ian. I agree that he's often an intolerable nuisance; and I think that without him this expedition would be much more businesslike and very gloomy indeed.

SHAWCROSS (*exasperated*)   The thing I admire most about you, M. F., is your wonderful broadmindedness. It's an example to me. I'm not very tolerant, I'm afraid. If Gunn amused you and the others, I'm glad. I hope I can see a joke as well as anyone . . . But that wasn't quite what I meant, just now. This is something quite different. I hardly like to tell you——

RANSOM   If you hadn't meant to tell me, you wouldn't have started this conversation at all.

SHAWCROSS (*blurting it out*)   Well then——Gunn steals!

RANSOM (*laughs*)   Oh, that!

SHAWCROSS   So you *did* know!

RANSOM   I'm surprised that you've only just noticed it. He steals like a magpie; bits of indiarubber, chiefly, but also watches, pencils, and, occasionally, money. . . . That reminds me, I expect he's taken my camera. I was imagining I'd lost it down in the gorge, while we were fording the river.

SHAWCROSS   But, M. F., you can't tolerate this kind of thing! What are you going to do?

RANSOM   Ask him if he's got it.

SHAWCROSS   But surely there's more to it than that? How can you take a man with you who's just a common thief? One has to have some standards of decency, I suppose?

RANSOM (*smiles*)   You haven't changed much, have you, Ian, since you were captain of your school?

SHAWCROSS (*bitterly*)   You're always laughing at me. I suppose you think I'm just a priggish fool.

RANSOM   I certainly don't think you're a fool. You know that I rely on your help more than anybody's to make this expedition a success.

SHAWCROSS   Thank you, M. F. You make me feel ashamed. As long as you trust me, then I don't give a damn what anybody else says or thinks. You know I'd follow you anywhere. We all would. . . . The wonderful thing about a man like you is that you can use all kinds of people and get the best out of each. I think I understand better now, what it is you get out of Gunn. I don't want to run him down—just because his brand of humour's a bit too subtle for me. (*With increasing bitterness*) He's not a bad sort in his way; he's all right to have about the place, I suppose, as long as there's no special difficulty or danger. He's a damn good climber too, I admit—only he simply hasn't got the temperament. I'm wondering what he'll be like up there, on the north face. You remember how he screamed, that day in the Coolins, and wouldn't budge for an hour? It was pitiful.

RANSOM   David's always frightened when he climbs. Otherwise, he wouldn't climb. Being frightened is his chief pleasure in life. He's frightened when he drives a racing-car or seduces somebody's wife. At present he prefers mountaineering because it frightens him most of all.

SHAWCROSS   How well you understand him, M. F. Now that's just the point I wanted to make: wouldn't it be better, when we get to Camp B, to leave Gunn behind?

RANSOM   (*smiles*)   To damage all the instruments and eat up all the stores?

SHAWCROSS   Well, but I mean, he'll have to be dropped somewhere, won't he? (*Pause*) Do you really think it's wise to take him as far as Camp A?

RANSOM   I shall decide when the time comes.

SHAWCROSS   I mean, it's quite settled, isn't it, that only two of us shall try to reach the summit?

RANSOM   Yes. There'll be only two of us.

SHAWCROSS   And you can't, for a moment, be thinking of taking Gunn? (*Pause*) My God, it'd be madness! M. F.—you couldn't!

RANSOM   Have I said I shall?

SHAWCROSS   (*with growing excitement*)   If I thought such a thing was possible, I'd—— I don't know what I'd do! Gunn,

that miserable little rotter! Why, he's not a climber at all!
He's just a neurotic! He poses. He does everything for ef-
fect! Just a beastly little posing coward! (*Pause*) Oh, I know
you think I'm simply jealous!
(*Enter* LAMP *and* DOCTOR, *L.*)

LAMP (*excited*)   The flora here is amazing, simply amazing!
I've had one of the most wonderful afternoons of my life!
I tell you what, Doctor——— (*Sees the others*) Oh, here
you are, M. F.! Didn't see you in the dark. (SHAWCROSS
silently lights the candles) I was just telling the doctor I've
had a field-day! Extraordinarily interesting! M. F., I'm convinced that Hawkins is wrong when he denies the possibility
of a five-leaved Polus Naufrangia! And what's more, I
don't mind betting you I shall find one here, on F 6.

RANSOM   Let's see what you got this afternoon.

LAMP (*opens his vasculum*)   Here's Stagnium Menengitis
and Frustrax Abominum. . . . Isn't it a beauty! And look
here, here's something to surprise you: you told me there
wasn't a Rossus Monstrens with blue petals! Well, what do
you say to this?

RANSOM (*examines flower*)   This is interesting.
(*Enter* GUNN, *L.*)

GUNN   Ah, here you all are! Thank goodness! I've been hunting for you everywhere! I began to think something had
happened to you. . . . (*Sits down and mops his forehead*)

DOCTOR   What's the matter with you, David? You look rattled.

GUNN   You'd be rattled if you'd been hanging round this
place all the afternoon. Ugh! It gives me the creeps!

DOCTOR   Why, what's wrong with it?

GUNN   Those beastly monks. . . . Don't they make you feel
damned queer with those cowls over their faces? I've been
watching them for hours out there; they never seem to
speak or make any signs; they just stand facing each other,
like this—and yet you have a nasty sort of feeling that
they're talking, somehow. . . . I shouldn't wonder if they
do it by telepathy or something.

DOCTOR   They seemed quite friendly and harmless when we
arrived.

GUNN   Don't you believe it. . . . They're plotting to do us in
while we're asleep, I bet you they are. . . . This afternoon,

when I was sitting watching the porters unload, I kept imagining there was somebody standing just behind me. Several times I turned round quickly to try and catch him, but there was nothing there. . . . And then I saw a monk and I thought I'd ask him which room we could use for the stores. So I went over to him and made signs and he seemed to understand all right. He turned round and went to one of the doors and opened it and went inside. Naturally, I followed him. But when I got into the room there was nobody there. And there wasn't even a window he could have got out of. . . . No, I don't like this place!

DOCTOR I tell you what, David, you've had a touch of the sun. I'll give you something to make you sleep well to-night.

RANSOM Oh, by the way, David, where's my camera? You've got it, haven't you?

GUNN (*with a charming smile*) Yes. It's in my room. I thought I'd look after it for you for a bit.

SHAWCROSS Well, of all the blasted——!

RANSOM That was very kind of you. Would you bring it here now, please?

GUNN Very well—if you'd rather——
(*As he moves towards the door L. a low chanting begins from the courtyard outside. This chant continues throughout the following scene. Its words are:*)

> Go Ga, morum tonga tara
> Mi no tang hum valka vara
> So so so kum mooni lara
>
> Korkra ha Chormopuloda
> Antifora lampisoda
> Kang ku gar, bari baroda
>
> Ming ting ishta sokloskaya
> No rum ga ga, no rum gaya
> Nong Chormopuloda sya.

GUNN My God! What's that? (*Retreats hastily behind* RANSOM'S *chair*)

SHAWCROSS (*goes to door L. and looks out*) They're all gathered out there in the courtyard. They're starting a procession. Now they're beginning to go round in circles. They've got torches and banners. . . .

GUNN   Lock that door, for Heaven's sake! Suppose they come in here!

SHAWCROSS   Do you ever think of anything except your own beastly little skin?
(*Meanwhile the others have joined him at the door.* GUNN *comes last, unwillingly, curious in spite of himself*)

DOCTOR   From the way they walk it might be a funeral.

LAMP   I believe it *is* a funeral. Look what they're carrying.

GUNN   A coffin! Gosh, did you see?

DOCTOR   Cheer up, David! There's only one. Perhaps they won't choose you.

GUNN   It's most likely some wretched traveller they've murdered.

DOCTOR   Very curious, those masks. A pity it's too dark for a photograph.

SHAWCROSS   Now they're going. I wonder where that door leads to? Probably into the temple precincts.
(*The chanting dies away*)

LAMP   (*as they close the door and return downstage to the table*)   What did you make of it, M. F.?

RANSOM   I've read about these rites, somewhere. They're supposed to propitiate the spirits which guard the house of the dead.

GUNN   Anyhow, I hope there won't be any more! Phew! This place is about as cheerful as Woking Cemetery! (*As he speaks, the door on the R. opens noiselessly and a cowled* MONK *enters, carrying in his hands a crystal which glows faintly with a bluish light*) You chaps didn't really think I was scared, did you? I was only ragging. It takes more than a few old monks to frighten *me!* (*Turns and suddenly sees the* MONK. *Screams*) Oh, God! (*As the* MONK *advances towards the front of the stage,* GUNN *retreats backwards before him*) What does he want? Help! Do something, somebody! M. F., you speak to him!

RANSOM   Om no hum, no na num se? (*Pause*) No num seng ka, gang se gang? (*Pause*) King t'sang po, ka no ah? (*Pause*) Either he doesn't understand any of the three hill-dialects, or he isn't allowed to answer.

DOCTOR   Funny kind of a lamp he's got there. (*Approaches*)

GUNN   I say! Do be careful! He may have a knife up his sleeve!

DOCTOR   Extraordinary thing—it doesn't seem to be a lamp at all. It just shines. (*Bends over the crystal*) Why, it's a kind of mirror—I can see myself in it! Am I really as fat as that? Gracious, I'm quite bald! Hullo, what's this? I'm sitting in an armchair. I seem to know that room. . . . Yes, it's the Reform Club! I say, I think I must have got a touch of the sun like David. Am I just seeing things? Here, Teddy, you come and look!

LAMP (*Looks*)   Polus Naufrangia! As plain as anything: all five leaves. By Jove, what a beauty! (*Rubs his eyes*) I must be going mad!

GUNN   He's hypnotising you, that's what it is! When we're all in a trance, we shall probably be murdered. . . . I say, I must have a look!

LAMP (*excited*)   I saw it as plain as that candle! Five distinct leaves!

GUNN (*looks*)   Why, there's my old Alfa Romeo! And someone's sitting in it—it's a woman, dressed all in black. She seems to be at a cross-roads. I see the sign-post, but I can't read what's written on it. . . . Now she's turning her head. My God, it's Toni—Mrs. da Silva! (*Comes away*) Do you think that means her husband's died and now she'll follow me out here? Come on, Ian. Your turn.

SHAWCROSS (*takes a pace towards the crystal, stops, bursts out violently*)   I'm not going to have anything to do with this damned business! You others please yourselves. It isn't right. We aren't meant to know these things. (*Calmer*) It's probably some kind of trick, anyhow . . . M. F., I'm going to get the wireless ready. It's nearly time to pick up the weather report from Fort George. (*Takes up one of the candles and—exits L.*)

GUNN   You'll have a look, won't you, M. F.?

RANSOM (*hesitates a moment*)   Very well. (*Looks into crystal*)
(*As he does so,* VOICES *are heard from the darkened Stage-Boxes*)

VOICES   Give me bread
                    Restore my dead
        I am sick

Help me quick

Give me a car

Make me a star

Make me neat

Guide my feet

Make me strong

Teach me where I belong

Strengthen my will

Make me still

Make me admired

Make me desired

Make me just

Cool my lust.

(*Together*)   Make us kind
Make us of one mind
Make us brave
Save
Save
Save
Save.

DOCTOR   Well, what is it this time? Motors or flowers or London clubs?

GUNN   Try and see something useful. Ask it to tell you the best route up F 6.

RANSOM   (*after a long pause*)   I can see nothing.

GUNN   Nothing at all? Oh, M. F.!

DOCTOR   That all goes to support your hypnotism theory. M. F. was a bit too strong for him.
(*The* MONK *turns silently and goes out by the door R.*)

GUNN   Ought we to have tipped him or anything? Gosh, you know, that crystal has given me quite a headache! I can't understand your not seeing anything, M. F. Or was it so awful that you won't tell us?

DOCTOR   I feel I could do with a change of air. Let's go and see if Ian's got Fort George.

GUNN   Right you are. Coming, M. F.?

RANSOM   No. I'll stay here. The Abbot may wish to speak to me.
(GUNN *and* DOCTOR *go out L.*)

RANSOM   Bring back the crystal. Let me look again and prove

my vision a poor fake. Was it to me they turned their rodent
faces, those ragged denizens of the waterfronts, and squealed
so piteously: "Restore us! Restore us to our uniqueness and
our human condition?" Was it for me the prayer of the sad
artist on the crowded beaches was indeed intended? "Assas-
sinate my horrible detachment. My love for these bathers
is hopeless and excessive. Make me also a servant." I
thought I saw the raddled sick cheeks of the world light up
at my approach as at the home-coming of an only son. . . .
How could I tell them that?

(*Enter the* ABBOT *and* TWO ACOLYTES, *R.*)

ABBOT (*makes sign of benediction*)   Only God is great.

RANSOM (*kneels and kisses his hand*)   But His power is for
mercy.

ABBOT   I hope everything has been arranged to your satisfaction?

RANSOM   It is perfect.

ABBOT   I am glad. Please be seated, Mr. Ranson. Will you
do me the honour of taking a glass of wine with me? In
these mountains, I fear we can offer but poor hospitality,
but I think you will not find this wine totally unworthy of
your palate. Your health, Mr. Ransom. (*Toast. The* ACO-
LYTES *exeunt R.*) Now tell me. You wish to start soon on
your ascension of our mountain?

RANSOM   To-morrow. If He permit it, Whose will must be
done.

ABBOT   You know the legend?

RANSOM   I have read the Book of the Dead.

ABBOT   Such interest, Mr. Ransom, is uncommon in one of
your race. In that case, you will have comprehended the
meaning of the ceremony that was performed this evening
out in the courtyard: the office for the souls of the dead
and the placation of the Demon. I am afraid that you, with
your Western civilisation, must consider us here excessively
superstitious. . . . No, you need not contradict me out of
politeness. I understand. You see the painted mask and the
horns and the eyes of fire and you think: "This Demon is
only a bogey that nurses use to frighten their children: I
have outgrown such nonsense. It is fit only for ignorant
monks and peasants. With our factory chimneys and our
furnaces and our locomotives we have banished these fairy-

tales. I shall climb the mountain and I shall see nothing."
But you would be wrong. The peasants, as you surmise
rightly, are simple and uneducated; so their vision is simple
and uneducated. They see the truth as a crude and coloured
picture. Perhaps, for that reason, they see it more clearly
than you or I. For it is a picture of truth. The Demon is
real. Only his ministry and his visitation are unique for
every nature. To the complicated and sensitive like yourself,
Mr. Ransom, his disguises are more subtle. He is—what
shall I say? the formless terror in the dream, the stooping
shadow that withdraws itself as you wake in the half-dawn.
You have heard his gnashing accusations in the high fever
at a very great distance. You have felt his presence in the
sinister contours of a valley or the sudden hostility of a copse
or the choking apprehension that fills you unaccountably
in the middle of the most intimate dinner-party. I did you
an injustice just now when I said that you expected to see
nothing on the mountain. You do expect to see something.
That is why you are intending to climb it. You do not make
that foolish, that terrible mistake so common among your
fellow-countrymen of imagining that it is fortunate to be
alive. No. You know, as I do, that Life is evil. You have
conquered the first temptation of the Demon, which is to
blind Man to his existence. But that victory exposes you to
a second and infinitely more dangerous temptation; the
temptation of pity; the temptation to overcome the Demon
by will. Mr. Ransom, I think I understand your temptation.
You wish to conquer the Demon and then to save mankind.
Am I right?

RANSOM   So you know of my vision in the crystal?

ABBOT   Ah, you saw it there, too? That is not strange. For
all men see reflected there some fragment of their nature
and glimpse a knowledge of those forces by whose free
operation the future is forecast and limited. That is not
supernatural. Nothing is revealed but what we have hidden
from ourselves; the treasure we have buried and accursed.
Your temptation, Mr. Ransom, is written in your face. You
know your powers and your intelligence. You could ask
the world to follow you and it would serve you with blind
obedience; for most men long to be delivered from the
terror of thinking and feeling for themselves. And yours
is the nature to which those are always attracted in whom
the desire for devotion and self-immolation is strongest.
And you would do them much good. Because men desire

evil, they must be governed by those who understand the corruption of their hearts, and can set bounds to it. As long as the world endures, there must be order, there must be government: but woe to the governors, for, by the very operation of their duty, however excellent, they themselves are destroyed. For you can only rule men by appealing to their fear and their lust; government requires the exercise of the human will: and the human will is from the Demon.

RANSOM   Supposing you are right. Supposing I abandon the mountain. What shall I do? Return to England and become a farm labourer or a factory hand?

ABBOT   You have gone too far for that.

RANSOM   Well then——

ABBOT   There is an alternative, Mr. Ransom; and I offer it to you.

RANSOM   What?

ABBOT   The complete abnegation of the will.

RANSOM   And that means——?

ABBOT   This. . . . (*Very quietly, during the preceding speech, the distant drum-beat of a funeral march has been heard. Through the above dialogue, it has grown steadily louder. A procession of* MONKS *now crosses the cloister at the back of the stage. They are bearing a number of fakirs in attitudes of asceticism; on litters, in coffins, impaled on spikes, etc. They cross from L. to R. and—exeunt*) Well, Mr. Ransom, I must leave you now. Do not make up your mind at once. Think my proposal over.

RANSOM   Before you go, may I ask you a question? As Abbot, you rule this monastery?

ABBOT   That is a wise observation. Mr. Ransom, I am going to tell you a secret which I have never told a living soul. We have spoken of your temptation. I am now going to tell you of mine. Sometimes, when I am tired or ill, I am subject to very strange attacks. They come without warning, in the middle of the night, in the noon siesta, even during the observance of the most sacred religious rites. Sometimes they come frequently, sometimes they do not occur for months or even years at a time. When they come I am filled with an intoxicating excitement, so that my hand trembles and all the hairs on my body bristle, and there comes suddenly into my mind strange words, snatches of song and even whole poems. These poems sing always of the same world. A strange world. The world of the common people. The world of blood and violent death, of peasant soldiers and murderers, of graves and disappointed lust. And when I come to myself again and see these monastery walls around me, I am filled with horror and despair. For I know that it is a visitation of the Demon. I know that, for me, nothing matters any more: it is too late. I am already among the lost. Good night, Mr. Ransom.

(*Exit R.*)

RANSOM   Is it too late for me? I recognise my purpose. There was a choice once, in the Lakeland Inn. I made it wrong; and if I choose again now, I must choose for myself alone, not for these others. Oh, You who are the history and the creator of all these forms in which we are condemned to suffer, to whom the necessary is also the just, show me, show each of us upon this mortal star the danger that under His hand is softly palpitating. Save us, save us from the destructive element of our will, for all we do is evil.

(*Enter* GUNN, *L.*)

GUNN   You alone? Good. I was afraid I might be butting in; but Ian and the others threw me out. And I didn't much like the idea of sitting by myself in the dark, with all those monks around. (*Pause*) Are you busy, M. F.? Would you rather I didn't talk? (RANSOM *is deep in his thoughts. He doesn't answer.* GUNN, *after regarding him for a moment in silence, begins again*) The wireless is coming through beautifully. No atmospherics at all. I heard the weather report; first class. We'll be able to start to-morrow for a cert.

RANSOM   You sound pleased.

GUNN   Of course I'm pleased! Who wouldn't be—after all these weeks of messing about? To-morrow we shall be on the ice!

RANSOM   Tell me, David; what is it that makes you so keen to climb this mountain?

GUNN   (*laughs*)   What is it that makes one keen to climb any mountain?

RANSOM   F 6 is not like any mountain you have ever climbed.

GUNN   Why not? It's got a top, hasn't it? And we want to get to it, don't we? I don't see anything very unusual in that.

RANSOM   You've thought enough about the ascent of F 6 no doubt; about the couloirs and the north buttress and the arrête. . . . Have you thought about the descent, too: the descent that goes down and down into the place where Stagmantle and my Brother and all their gang are waiting? Have you thought about the crowds in the streets down there, and the loud-speakers and the posing and the photographing and the hack-written articles you'll be paid thousands to sign? Have you smelt the smell of their ceremonial banquets? Have you loathed them, and even as you were loathing them, begun to like it all? (*Becomes hysterically excited*) Have you? Have you?

GUNN (*scared*)   M. F., what on earth do you mean?

RANSOM   Don't lie to me now, David. Are you corrupt, like the rest of us? I must know. (*Seizes* GUNN *by the wrists and stares into his face*) Yes. Yes. I see it! You too. How horrible! (*Throws him violently aside*) Get out of my sight! (*Enter* SHAWCROSS, DOCTOR *and* LAMP; *all far too excited to notice that anything unusual has been happening*)

SHAWCROSS   M. F.! A message has just come through: Blavek and his party are on the mountain already!

GUNN   But it's impossible! When we last heard, he was still on the other side of the Tung Desert!

SHAWCROSS   Well, this is official. He must have been making forced marches. These fellows aren't mountaineers at all— they're soldiers! There's a whole regiment of them! Do you know, M. F., what they're doing? They're hammering the whole south face full of pitons and hauling each other up like sacks! Good God, they'll be using fire-escapes before they've finished! Well, that settles it! We haven't a moment to lose!

RANSOM   And you are all anxious to play their game; the race to the summit? This won't be mountaineering. It'll be a steeplechase. Are you so sure the prize is worth it? Ian, you're the purist: is this your idea of climbing? No time for observations; no time for reconnoitre? Teddy, hadn't you better stay out of this? We can't wait a week, you know, while you look for your flowers.

LAMP   I'll take my chance of that later. We've got to beat Blavek!

RANSOM   Blavek is only another victim of the mountain. And you, Tom?

DOCTOR   You don't expect me to stay here, do you, M. F.? Why, this makes me feel twenty years younger already!

M.C.   We've cut the Dies Irae, your Majesty.

KING   Good. I'm so glad you agree with me. I heard several complaints last time, that it was too gruesome. As you know, I am particularly anxious not to hurt anybody's feelings. It's a beautiful piece, of course, but one can't expect them to be quite educated up to it yet. One has to make allowances. . . . Oh, and by the way, you might tell the male alto to moderate his top notes a bit. Last time, he gave the Queen a headache.

M.C.   I will, your Majesty.

KING   Excellent. Then I think we can begin. Bring in the prisoners. (*To the* QUEEN) My dear, your crown is a little crooked. Allow me.
(*Solemn music. The* PRISONERS, *with their wives and mothers, are brought in. The* PRISONERS *are workmen, dressed neatly in their Sunday clothes. The women, like the ladies of the court, are dressed in black*)

CHOIR   Requiem aeternam dona et lux perpetua luceat eis.

KING   (*rising to address the* PRISONERS)   Gentlemen. I do not intend to keep you long; but I cannot let this opportunity slip by without saying how much I and the Queen appreciate and admire the spirit in which you have acted and how extremely sorry we both are that our little differences can only be settled in this er . . . somewhat drastic fashion.
    Believe me, I sympathise with your aims from the bottom of my heart. Are we not all socialists nowadays? But as men of the world I am sure you will agree with me that order has to be maintained. In spite of everything which has happened, I do want us to keep this solemn moment free from any thought of malice. If any of you have a complaint to make about your treatment, I hope you will say so now before it is too late. You haven't? I am very glad indeed to hear it. Before going on to the next part of the ceremony, let me conclude by wishing you Bon Voyage and every happiness in the next world.
(*Music. The* PRISONERS *are led out. A footman brings a gold revolver on a cushion and presents it to the* KING, *who follows the* PRISONERS)

CANTOR   Kyrie eleison.

CHOIR   Mars eleison.

CANTOR   Kyrie eleison.

CANTOR Homo natus de muliere, brevi vivens tempore, repletur multis miseriis. Qui quasi flos egreditur et conteritur et fugit velut umbra, et nunquam in eodem statu permanet.

Media via in morte sumus: quem quaerimus adjutorem nisi te, Domine, qui pro peccatis nostris juste irasceris?

Sancte Zeus, sancto fortis, sancte et misericors Salvator amaris mortis aeternae poenis ne tradas nos. Mars omnipotens. Frater Jovis, qui tollis peccata mundi.

CHOIR Miserere nobis.

CANTOR Qui tollis peccata mundi.

CHOIR Miserere nobis.

CANTOR Qui tollis peccata mundi.

CHOIR Suscipe deprecationem nostram.

CANTOR Qui sedet ad dextram Jovis.

CHOIR Miserere nobis.
(*Shots are heard, off. The Last Post is sounded*)

CHOIR Proficiscere Anima Ostniana, de hoc mundo.
(*Re-enter the* KING. *A footman brings a silk handkerchief to clean the revolver. Another footman brings a basin of water and a towel. The* KING *washes his hands. The four corpses are brought in on stretchers*)

CHOIR Rex tremendae majestatis, qui salvandos salvas gratis salva me fons pietatis.
(*Trumpet*)

M.C. Her Majesty the Queen will now address the bereaved.

QUEEN (*to the wives and mothers of the* PRISONERS) Ladies (or may I call you Sisters?). On this day of national sorrow, my woman's heart bleeds for you. I too am a mother. I too have borne the pangs of childbirth and known the unutterable comfort of seeing a little curly head asleep on my breast. I too am a wife and have lain in the strong arms of the beloved. Remember, then, in your loss, that in all you suffer, I suffer with you. And remember that Suffering is Woman's fate and Woman's glory. By suffering we are ennobled; we rise to higher things. Be comforted, therefore, and abide patiently, strong in the hope that you will meet your loved ones again in another and better world where there are no tears, no pains, no misunderstandings; where we shall all walk hand in hand from everlasting to everlasting.

M.C.   The ladies of the Court will offer the bereaved some
light refreshment.
(*The* LADIES *take round champagne and cakes to the* PRIS-
ONERS' WOMEN)

A WOMAN (*with a sudden hysterical scream*)   Murderers!!
(*All the* WOMEN *are instantly and politely removed by footmen. The* COURTIERS *cough and look at the ceiling in pained
embarrassment*)

KING   Poor things! They don't really mean it, you know.

QUEEN   They lead such terrible lives!
(*All the* COURTIERS *sigh deeply. The* LADIES *of the court
begin to admire the corpses*)

1ST LADY   How lovely they look:
Like pictures in a children's book!

2ND L.   Look at this one. He seems so calm,
As if he were asleep with his head in his arm.
He's the handsomest, don't you think, of the four?
How I wish I'd met him before!
I'll put some blood on my hanky, a weeny spot,
So that he never shall be forgot.

3RD L.   Oh Duchess, isn't he just a duck!
His fiancée certainly had the luck.
He can't have been more than nineteen, I should say.
He must have been full of Vitamin A.

2ND L.   Dear Lady Emily,
What a clever simile!

4TH L.   What beautiful hair; as white as wool!
And such strong hands. Why, they're not yet cool!
Lend me a pair of scissors, dear.
I want a lock as a souvenir.

M.C.   Three Englishmen crave an audience with your Majesty.

KING   Oh, certainly, certainly. I'll see them at once.
(*Trumpet*)

M.C.   Mr. Alan Norman and friends.
(*Enter* ALAN *and the two* JOURNALISTS. *They kiss the* KING'S
hand)

KING   How do you do? Delighted to see anyone from England. I have very happy memories of visits there before the
War. The singing in King's Chapel was marvellous, quite
marvellous. And Melba, ah, delicious! Talking of which, I

hope you liked our singing today? I'm always most grateful for any criticisms. . . . How's London? My dear London! Those evenings at the Crystal Palace! What a building! What fireworks! I hear Regent Street is quite unrecognizable now. Dear me, how time flies, hm, indeed, yes. . . . But I mustn't bore you with an old man's memories. What can I do for you?

ALAN   I'm looking for Sir Francis Crewe:
      Is his name, Sire, known to you?

KING   Sir Francis Crewe? Hm, let me think. He wasn't one of your ambassadors, by any chance? I'm so stupid about names. (*To the* MASTER OF CEREMONIES) Ask the Court if they know anything about an Englishman called Sir Francis Crewe.
(*Trumpet*)

M.C.   Is an Englishman, Sir Francis Crewe,
      Familiar to anyone of you?
(*Silence*)

KING   You see? I'm so sorry. . . . But I tell you what: You might try the Red Light District. It's always full of foreign visitors. (*To* M.C.) Is the Crown Prince in?

M.C.   No, your Majesty.

KING   What a pity. He'd have been delighted to show you around. He's always going down there. It worries the Queen dreadfully, but I tell her not to take it to heart so: Boys will be boys. . . . Have you got a plan of the city?

M.C.   Here's one, your Majesty.

KING   Thanks. (*Opening the plan, to* ALAN) Come round on this side, you'll see better. Here's the Palace and here's the Palace Underground Station, just opposite. You take the tube to the Triangle: It's a two angel fare, I think. Then you take a number four tram to the Butter Kiln. After that, I'm afraid you'll have to walk. Keep left at the Cemetery.

M.C.   Excuse me, your Majesty, but the trams aren't running and everything's shut because of the executions.

KING   Of course! How silly of me to forget! Ring up the Broadcasting Station at once and have the mourning called off.
(M.C. *bows and retires*)

KING Well, goodbye, and I hope you find your friend. I'm
   sorry we couldn't do more for you. . . . By the by, are you
   sure you didn't see anything in the least bit out of taste in
   our ceremony? I always think the English have such good
   taste in matters of ritual. You didn't? That's very encour-
   aging. When you get back to England, remember me to Lord
   Harborne, if he's still alive. One of the real old English
   eccentrics. Used to breakfast at midnight on champagne and
   raw beef. . . . Won't you have a drink before you go?

ALAN No thank you, your Majesty. You see, we haven't got
   much time.

KING Well, goodbye. Goodbye. (*Aside to the* M.C. *crossly*)
   What on earth is the band-master thinking of? Tell him to
   play something suitable at once, in honour of our guests.
   (*As* ALAN *and the* JOURNALISTS *retire backwards, bowing,
   the band begins to play "Rule, Britannia"*)

CURTAIN

Chorus

You with shooting-sticks and cases for field-glasses, your limou-
      sines parked in a circle: who visit the public games, ob-
      serving in burberries the feats of the body:
You who stand before the west fronts of cathedrals: appraising
      the curious carving:
The virgin creeping like a cat to the desert, the trumpeting
      angels, the usurers boiling:
And you also who look for truth: alone in tower:
Follow our hero and his escort on his latest journey: From the
      square surrounded by Georgian houses, taking the lurch-
      ing tram eastward
South of the ship-cranes, of the Slythe canal: Stopping at
      Fruby and Drulger Street,
Past boys ball-using: shrill in alleys.
Passing the cinemas blazing with bulbs: bowers of bliss
Where thousands are holding hands: they gape at the tropical
      vegetation, at the Ionic pillars and the organ solo.
Look left: The moon shows locked sheds, wharves by water,
On your right is the Power House: its chimneys fume gently
      above us like rifles recently fired.

Look through the grating at the vast machinery: at the dyna-
  mos and turbines
Grave, giving no sign of the hurricane of steam within their
  huge steel bottles,
At the Diesel engines like howdahed elephants: at the dials
  with their flickering pointers:
Power to the city: where loyalties are not those of the family.
And now, enter:
O human pity, gripped by the crying of a captured bird wincing
  at sight of surgeon's lance,
Shudder indeed: that life on its narrow littoral so lucky
Can match against eternity a time so cruel!
The street we enter with setts is paved: cracked and uneven as
  an Alpine glacier,
Garbage chucked in the gutters has collected in the hollows in
  loathsome pools,
Back to back houses on both sides stretch: a dead-straight line
  of dung-colored brick
Wretched and dirty as a run for chickens.
Full as a theatre is the foul thoroughfare: some sitting like
  sacks, some slackly standing,
Their faces grey in the glimmering gaslight: their eyeballs
  drugged like a dead rabbit's,
From a window a child is looking, by want so fretted his face
  has assumed the features of a tortoise:
A human forest: all by one infection cancelled.
Despair so far invading every tissue has destroyed in these the
  hidden seat of the desire and the intelligence.

A little further, and now: Enter the street of some of your
  dreams:
Here come the untidy jokers and the spruce who love military
  secrets
And those whose houses are dustless and full of Ming vases:
Those rebels who have freed nothing in the whole universe
  from the tyranny of the mothers, except a tiny sensitive
  area:
Those who are ashamed of their baldness or the size of their
  members,
Those suffering from self-deceptions necessary to life
And all who have compounded envy and hopelessness into
  desire
Perform here nightly their magical acts of identification
Among the Chinese lanterns and the champagne served in
  shoes.

You may kiss what you like; it has often been kissed before.
Use what words you wish; they will often be heard again.

Scene V

(*Ostnia. A street in the Red Light District. Each café has a small lighted peep-hole, resembling a theatre box-office. Above each of the four peep-holes is a sign-board with the name:* TIGER JACK'S. YAMA THE PIT. COSY CORNER. MOTHER HUBBARD'S. *The heads of the four proprietors are visible at the peep-holes*)

FOUR PROPRIETORS (*singing together*)
> To Red Lamp Street you are all invited;
> Here Plato's halves are at last united.
> Whatever you dream of alone in bed,
> Come to us and we will make it real instead.

TIGER JACK   Do you feel like a bit of fun?
> At Tiger Jack's you will find it done.
> We've girls of eighty and women of four;
> Let them teach you things you never knew before.

PROPRIETRESS OF YAMA THE PIT
> Or does the thought of a thorough whipping
> By ladies in boots set your pulses skipping.
> At Yama the Pit you must pay a call
> And soon you won't be able to sit down at all.

BOSS OF COSY CORNER
> But perhaps you're a woman-scorner?
> Then step inside at the Cosy Corner.
> We've boys of every shape and size:
> Come and gaze into their great big eyes.

MOTHER HUBBARD   If you've taken a fancy to snow,
> Mother Hubbard's the place to go.
> With Cokey Minnie and Dopey Jim
> You can hold a party till the stars are dim.

ALL TOGETHER   Ladies and gentlemen, bear in mind
> Kisses in the graveyard are hard to find.
> "Tempus fugit," the poet said:
> So come to us at once for you will soon be dead.

(Enter ALAN, *the* JOURNALISTS *and the* DOG. *They are immediately accosted by two touts. The* 1ST TOUT *is very old and bleary. The* 2ND TOUT *is a boy of eight)*

1ST T.   Buy a post-card, guvnor?

2ND T.   Come wiv me. Good Jig-a-Jig.

ALAN *(going up to* TIGER JACK*)*
          Good evening. Is Sir Francis Crewe,
          English, known perhaps to you?

TIGER JACK   Money, money
          Makes our speech as sweet as honey.
    (ALAN *gives money*)
          Now ask again
          And not in vain.

ALAN   Good evening. Is Sir Francis Crewe,
          English, known perhaps to you?

TIGER JACK   Phyllis, Lou,
          All of you,
          Have you heard of Sir Francis Crewe?

VOICES *(from within)*   A Francis I knew
          (a nice boy, too)
          And I a Crewe.
          But none of us know Sir Francis Crewe.

TIGER JACK   But stay.
          Here it is gay.

ALAN   No thank you, no.
          I must go.
    (Moves on)

1ST TOUT   Buy a post-card, guvnor?

2ND T.   Come wiv me. Good Jig-a-Jig.

ALAN *(to* PROPRIETRESS OF YAMA THE PIT*)*
          Good evening. Is Sir Francis Crewe,
          English, known perhaps to you?

PROPRIETRESS OF Y. P.   Money, money
          Makes our speech as sweet as honey.
    (ALAN *gives money*)
          You must pay more.
    (ALAN *gives more*)
          Now speak again,
          Not in vain.

ALAN   Good evening. Is Sir Francis Crewe,
          English, known perhaps to you?

PROPRIETRESS OF Y. P.   Sue, Sue,
          That will do!
          He's already black and blue.
          Have you heard of Sir Francis Crewe?

SUE'S VOICE   I had an Englishman last year
          Who wore a pendant in each ear,
          Then there was one with a false nose:
          It wasn't either of them, I suppose?
          But stay,
          Here it is gay.

ALAN   No thank you, no.
          I must go.
   (*Moves away*)

1ST TOUT   Buy a post-card, guvnor?
   (2ND J. *buys one*)

1ST J.   (*looking at it over his shoulder, in disgust*)
          Horrible hips and too much flesh:
          Why can't they get hold of someone fresh?

2ND T.   Come wiv me. Good Jig-a-Jig.

ALAN   (*giving money to the* BOSS OF COSY CORNER)
          Good evening. Is Sir Francis Crewe,
          English, known perhaps to you?

BOSS OF C.C.
          You speak English? But I too!
          Am I acquaint with Sir Francis Crewe?
          Every English Lord come here.
          Is it he in the corner there?
          Wait a moment while I send
          For Willy. . . . Willy,
          How calls himself your English friend?

WILLY'S VOICE
          Harold. . . . Have you a cigarette for me?

BOSS OF C.C.   Is it he?
          Well, come inside and wait and see.
          Many come in after ten.
          Perhaps he will be one of them.

ALAN   No thank you, no.
          I must go.
   (*Moves away*)

1ST J.   Remember the sign.

2ND T.   Come wiv me. Good Jig-a-Jig.

(1ST J. *chases him away*)

2ND T.   And say the line.
(ALAN *knocks three times at the door of* MOTHER HUB-
BARD'S)

MOTHER HUBBARD   The cupboard was bare.

ALAN   And yet the poor dog got some.
(*Gives money*)
Is the name Sir Francis Crewe,
English, known perhaps to you?

MOTHER HUBBARD
Wait a moment, please. I'll get Dopey Jim.
(*She disappears*)

1ST JOURNALIST   Hurry, hurry, do!
Our train leaves for Westland at twenty to.

2ND J.   Chuck up hunting for your boy friend.
It's clear that he's come to a sticky end.
(*The face of a drug addict, hopelessly dazed, appears at the
peep-hole*)

ALAN   Good evening. Are you Mr. Dopey Jim?

ADDICT   That's what they call me here: Up there, in the
world, I had another name. For I could dance lightly and
spring high like a rubber ball in the air: being champion at
Flash Green of all such sports.

ALAN   You know Flash Green? Why, that's where Sorbo
Lamb came from! He went away seven years ago to look for
Sir Francis Crewe. Did you ever meet him?

ADDICT   My mother bore no twins.

ALAN   Sorbo!

ADDICT   Alas.

ALAN   Oh, I am so glad! Whatever are you doing here? Have
you seen Francis? Come along, we'll look for him together.

ADDICT   I may not leave this place.

ALAN   Do you mean they won't let you out? We'll soon see
about that! There's four of us, and my dog can fight like a
tiger. Just let them try to stop you!

ADDICT You do not understand. (*Holds up his hands, which are free*) Don't you see these chains? My punishment and my reward. The light of your world would dazzle me and its noises offend my ears. Fools! How could you possibly appreciate my exquisite pleasures? Sometimes I lie quite still for days together, contemplating the flame of a candle or the oscillating shadow of a lamp. What revelations, what bottomless despairs! Please leave me alone.

ALAN Sorbo. . . . Isn't there anything I can do?

ADDICT Yes. Tell them at Flash Green that I am dead. More I ask not. Farewell.
(*He disappears*)

ALAN What shall I do? What shall I do?
  I cannot find Sir Francis Crewe!

2ND J. Pull your socks up, kid, and don't make a fuss!
  Come along to Westland now with us.
  Your friend may be there: You never know:
  And we'll show you all there is to show.
(*All three exeunt with* DOG, *singing*)
  If yer wants to see me agyne
    Then come to the stytion before the tryne.
  In the general wytin' 'all
    We'll see each other fer the very las' time of all!
(*The* FOUR PROPRIETORS *sing, accompanied by* FIRST TOUT *on the concertina and* SECOND TOUT *on the penny whistle*)

ALL TOGETHER
  Let us remember in a little song
  Those who were with us but not for long.
  Some were beautiful and some were gay
  But Death's Black Maria took them all away.

TIGER JACK
  Lucky Lil got a rope of pearls,
  Olive had autographed letters from earls,
  Grace looked lovely when she danced the Fern
  But Death took them yachting and they won't return.

YAMA THE PIT
  Prixie had a baron as a customer,
  He bought a zeppelin, just for her.
  You should have seen her with a hunting crop,
  But in Death's sound-proof room she's got to stop.

COSY CORNER
  Tony the Kid looked a god in shorts,

Phil was asked to Switzerland for winter sports,
Jimmy sent them crazy in his thick white socks,
But Death has shut them all up in a long black box.

MOTHER HUBBARD
Sammy and Di beat the gong round,
Wherever they walked there was snow on the ground.
Jessie and Colin had rings round their eyes
But Death put them where they can't get supplies.

ALL TOGETHER
When we are dead we shan't thank for flowers,
We shan't hear the parson preaching for hours,
We shan't be sorry to be white bare bone
At last we shan't be hungry and can sleep alone.

CURTAIN

Act Two

Scene 1

(*Westland. A room in a lunatic asylum. At the back of the stage is a large portrait of a man in uniform: beneath which is written "Our Leader." The man has a loud-speaker instead of a face. The room is full of lunatics, male and female, who sit on their beds absorbed in various occupations or wander up and down the stage. On meeting each other, they exchange the Westland Salute: bringing the palm of the right hand smartly against the nape of the neck. Their manner is furtive and scared*)

1ST MAD LADY (*wanders across the stage, singing*)
> Seen when night was silent,
> The bean-shaped island
> And our ugly comic servant
> Who is observant
> O the verandah and the fruit
> The tiny steamer in the bay
> Startling summer with its hoot.
> You have gone away.

1ST LUNATIC (*whispering with* 2ND LUNATIC *in a corner*) Heard any rumours?

2ND L. Heaps!

1ST L. Oh, do tell me!

2ND L. Ssh! not so loud. I think they may be watching us.

1ST L. I tell you what: I've got a plan. We'll say goodbye now and then meet later, as if by accident.

2ND L. All right. But do be careful.
(*They exchange the Westland Salute and separate to their respective beds*)

(*Enter* TWO MEDICAL OFFICERS *with* ALAN *in a strait-waist-coat, in a wheeled chair*)

1ST M.O.   The Ostnia Frontier, wasn't it? They've sent us several beauties.

2ND M.O.   Yes.

1ST M.O.   What do they say?

2ND M.O.   Travelling with a dog.

1ST M.O.   Hm. Canophilia.

1ST M.O.   States he is looking for someone he doesn't know.

2ND M.O.   Phantasy Building. Go on.

1ST M.O.   Doesn't know the Westland Song.

2ND M.O.   Amnesia. Pretty serious. (*To* ALAN) Now you. Have you ever been to the North Pole?

ALAN   No.

1ST M.O.   Can you speak Chinese?

ALAN   No!

2ND M.O.   Do you dye your hair?

ALAN   No!

1ST M.O.   Was your mother a negress?

ALAN   No!!

2ND M.O.   Do you drink your bathwater?

ALAN   No!!!

1ST M.O.   Do you like my face?

ALAN   (*losing his temper and yelling*)   No!!!!

1ST M.O.   Just as I feared, a typical case of negativism.

ALAN   What are you going to do? Let me out of here.

2ND M.O.   The gag, I think, don't you?

1ST M.O.   Yes, I think so.
   (*They gag* ALAN)

2ND M.O.   Quite classic. He'll be an ornament to our collection.
   (*Exeunt* MEDICAL OFFICERS)

2ND MAD LADY (*promenading with* 3RD M.L.)   The Leader says that next year he's going to put all us women into coops,

like hens. And if we don't lay properly we shall be fattened for the Christmas Market.

3RD M.L.   Oh, what a lovely idea!

2ND M.L.   Yes, isn't it? And so beautiful, too. I mean, it will
really make Motherhood sacred. And do away with all this
horrible unwomanly nonsense about girls being independent.
I'm sure *I* never wanted to be independent!

3RD M.L.   I should think not, indeed! (*Shivers*) Ugh, the
idea!
(*Several* LUNATICS *surround a* LUNATIC *who is naked except
for a bath-towel round his waist and has covered his body
with smears of ink*)

NAKED LUNATIC   I am the President of the newly-formed
League of the Forefathers of Westland, which the Leader
himself has officially approved. After careful historical investigations, I have discovered that this is the exact costume
worn by the inhabitants of Westland two thousand years
ago. All modern dress is effeminate and foreign. The L.F.W.
will lead Westland back to the manly customs of our ancestors. Down with Machinery! Down with knives and forks!
Down with bath-rooms and books! Let us take to the woods
and live on roots!
(*The other* LUNATICS, *in great excitement, begin tearing off
their clothes and scratching on the floor, as if to dig up
plants from the ground. Meanwhile, the* 1ST *and* 2ND *LUNA-
TICS leave their beds and greet each other with much ceremony*)

1ST L.   Ah, good morning, my dear Baron!

2ND L.   Your Worship, this is indeed a pleasure!

1ST L.   Remarkably mild weather, is it not?

2ND L.   (*in the same tone of voice, nodding his head slightly
in the direction of one of the other* LUNATICS)   I hear the
Admiral is going to be denounced.

1ST L.   (*obviously delighted*)   Oh, I'm so sorry! Poor fellow!
What for?

2ND L.   The usual. Byzantinism, of course: and Disaffection
and Hoarding.

1ST L.   Tut, tut! I should never have believed it of him!

2ND L.   Oh, he's got a bad record. They say there's more
than two thousand anonymous letters been written complaining about him to the Secret Police. *And all in invisible ink!*

1ST L.   Whew, that's nasty! (*Gleefully*) What do you think they'll do with him?

2ND L.   Send him to the Lead Mines, I expect.

1ST L.   (*rubbing his hands together*)   Poor fellow!
(LUNATIC, *who has just fastened a flag to the end of his bed, shouts across to the* LUNATIC *sitting on the bed opposite*)

FLAG-LUNATIC   Hi, you! Why haven't you got your flag out? Don't you know what today is?

LUNATIC WITHOUT FLAG   Of course I do! It's the Day of National Rejoicing.

FLAG-L.   Then why don't you hang out your flag? If your flag isn't out, you can't be rejoicing.

L. WITHOUT F.   Of course I'm rejoicing. I was just sitting rejoicing quietly by myself when you disturbed me.

FLAG-L.   I don't believe you're rejoicing a bit! You don't look as if you were rejoicing.

L. WITHOUT F.   Well, neither do you, for that matter.

FLAG-L.   It doesn't matter how I look. I've got my flag out. Everyone knows *I'm* rejoicing.

L. WITHOUT F.   What are you rejoicing about?

FLAG-L.   I shan't tell you. What are you?

L. WITHOUT F.   I shan't tell you either.

FLAG-L.   Oh yes you will!

L. WITHOUT F.   No I won't!

FLAG-L.   Will!

L. WITHOUT F.   Won't!
(*The two* LUNATICS *adopt threatening attitudes and make horrible faces at each other*)
(*A trumpet*)

1ST LUNATIC   Silence everybody! The Leader is going to speak to us!
(*All the* LUNATICS *stand up and give the Westland Salute*)

THE VOICE OF THE LEADER (*through the loud-speaker in the picture*)   A short time ago, I was spending a week-end at a little village in the mountains. I sat on the verandah of the simple old Westland inn, looking out across the street to the meadows and the mountains beyond, those snow-capped peaks already flushed with the sunset glow. Westland swallows swooped in and out of the eaves overhead. In a doorway opposite, a young mother looked down at her suckling babe with ineffable Westland tenderness. In another, a Westland granny gazed out into the dusk with perfect serenity on her beautiful old face. Sturdy rosy-cheeked Westland youngsters romped in the new-mown hay a little further off. And presently down the street came the returning cattle, all their bells a-chiming in a sweet symphony, followed by the peasants, so honest, so thrifty, so frugal, wedded to the dear Westland earth in an eternal, holy marriage.

(*The* LUNATICS *have been much affected by this part of the speech. They sigh, shed tears and embrace each other with loud smacking kisses. One of the male lunatics takes flowers from a vase and distributes them among the ladies, who put the flowers in their hair*)

VOICE OF THE LEADER (*continuing*)   My eyes filled with tears. I could not speak just then. Perish the man, I thought, who can imagine this people capable of any base or unworthy deed! Westland! *Our* Westland! *My* Westland! All, all mine!

BUT:

A chill struck my heart. There *was* a shadow!

Not two hundred miles from where I stand, there is a Nation: trained to arms from infancy, schooled in military obedience and precision, saluting even in the cradle, splendidly equipped with every invention of modern science, able, resolute, taught to regard the individual as nothing and the State as all, scorning treaties as mere scraps of paper to be rent asunder when the interests of the State demand. My mind's eye saw the long silent grey ranks. I heard the shouting of the captains, the brazen call of the trumpet and the pawing of the chargers. And a voice said: Woe, woe to the unprepared: For their inheritance shall be taken away and their home be left desolate! (*The* LUNATICS *are now violently agitated. Some of them moan and shiver with fear, lie flat on the floor or crawl under the beds. Others blow trumpets, wave toy swords and strike down imaginary enemies*) From how slight a cause may proceed terrifying results! A piece of paper left by a picnic party which has inadvertently strayed over the frontier, a rash word in a letter about the superiority of Westland beer or a humorous sketch in a revue misunderstood: and in a moment it is too late. Destruction might come upon us like a thief in the night: while you are innocently dozing in your chair, or making an omelette or washing dishes at the kitchen sink. A secret cabinet meeting, a word whispered into the telephone and within half an hour, within twenty minutes, the black hordes of death are darkening the Westland air with their horrible shadows.

Picture the scene, Oh mothers! Your baby's face, pinched and puckered: Not by hunger, no. Sated with poison from the air it breathes, its tender little mouth agape, choking up froth and green bile.

Sons, see your aged father who has taught you to reverence truth and purity: see him caught as the house collapses, his skull smashed like an egg before your eyes by a falling beam!

Think, teachers, of the bombs falling suddenly in the playing-field! There goes that splendid young forward . . . ah! he's down: collapsing even as he reaches the goal-post, his beautiful hinged limbs contracted in agony!

(*Most of the* LUNATICS *are now staring up at the ceiling in fascinated horror, as though awaiting the aeroplanes' arrival*)

VOICE OF THE LEADER (*continuing*) Nor is this all. The flame once lit would spread into a universal conflagration. England, Iceland, Ecuador and Siam would flare and within a week our civilisation, all that our statesmen and thinkers, our poets and musicians, have travailed for down the ages of history, would lie a smoking ruin!

No, this must not be! Westland is the guardian of Europe. We love peace (I say it in absolute confidence) more than any other country. Let us be ready and able to enforce it. We must build an air force of such a magnitude that any enemy, however ferocious, will think twice before daring to strike. Within three weeks we must have a million planes, not one less! We must make a stupendous effort. No sacrifice is too great. I expect every man, woman and child in Westland to help. Give up that cigar after lunch, do without an extra lipstick, abstain from your favourite sweets. Is that too much to ask when the safety of the Homeland is at stake? Our responsibilities are vast: Let us be worthy of them. And God help us all.

(*Tremendous enthusiasm. The* LUNATICS *jump up and down in their delight, cheer, embrace, pillow-fight, and box each other's ears*)

THE LUNATIC WITH THE FLAG Let's build a great big plane for our Leader!

LUNATICS   Oh yes! Let's!!

(*The* LUNATICS *begin dragging beds together and piling fur-niture upon them. The din is tremendous. Suddenly, at the window, appear the heads of the* TWO JOURNALISTS *and the* DOG. *They peer cautiously into the room, looking for* ALAN. *After a moment, they hastily withdraw*)

1ST LUNATIC (*who evidently considers himself the most im-portant of them all and is rather piqued that the plane-build-ing should have been suggested by someone else, stands on a chair and begins clapping his hands to command attention; after some time, he succeeds in getting the* LUNATICS *to stop working and listen to him*)   Madmen of Westland!

In this hour of supreme crisis, I feel called upon to say a few words. This is my message to you all. Let us never forget that we are Westlanders first and madmen second. As West-landers, we have a great tradition to uphold. Westland has always produced ten per cent. more lunatics than any other country in Europe. And are we going to show ourselves in-ferior to our forefathers? Never!

(*The* JOURNALISTS *reappear at the window, try the strength of the bars and shake their heads. The* DOG *is seen arguing with them in dumb show and indicating that they come with him. They all disappear*)

1ST LUNATIC (*continuing*)   Of recent years, there have ap-peared in our midst, masquerading as men of science, cer-tain Jews, obscurantists and Marxist traitors. These men have published enormous books, attempting to provide new classifications and forms of lunacy. But we are not deceived. No foreign brand of madness, however spectacular, how-ever noisy or pleasant, will ever seduce us from the grand old Westland Mania. What was good enough for our forefathers, we declare, is good enough for us! We shall continue to go mad in the time-honoured Westland way.

A LUNATIC   Three cheers for the Westland Loonies!

ALL   Hurrah! Hurrah! Hurrah!

ANOTHER LUNATIC (*suddenly seeing* ALAN)   Hullo, you! Why don't you cheer?

(*All the* LUNATICS *stop shouting and look at* ALAN. *At this moment, unseen by any of them, the* TWO JOURNALISTS *enter the room by a door on the right of the stage*)

ANOTHER LUNATIC   His mouth's tied up! He's got the tooth-ache!

(*Begins to giggle*)

ANOTHER LUNATIC He's been sent here to spy on us!

ANOTHER He's been hoarding butter!

ANOTHER He's insulted the Leader!

ANOTHER Rumour-monger!

ANOTHER Non-Aryan!

ANOTHER Separatist!

ANOTHER Grumbler!
(*All this time, they draw closer to him, rushing forward in turns to tug at his hair, tweak his nose or pull his ears*)

A LUNATIC Squirt water at him!

ANOTHER Put a rat in his bed!

ANOTHER Tickle his toes!

ANOTHER Shave off his eyebrows!

ANOTHER I say, chaps! Let's do something really exciting! Let's put lavatory paper under his chair and burn it!
(*They seem about to make a final rush at* ALAN, *when the* JOURNALIST *speaks, in a very loud and impressive voice, like a conjurer*)

1ST J. Ladies and Gentlemen! (*All the* LUNATICS *turn round to stare at him*) I am about to show you a simple but extremely interesting scientific experiment. (*Holds up his hand*) Now, watch the duck's head and please keep absolutely still while I count a hundred. One. Two. Three. . . .
(*While the* 1ST JOURNALIST *is counting, the* 2ND JOURNALIST, *on all fours, worms his way through the crowd to* ALAN'S *side and begins hastily undoing the ropes and straps*)

2ND J. (*in a low voice, to* ALAN) Gosh, that was a close shave!

ALAN How on earth did you find me?

2ND J. Your dog guided us here. That animal is better than the whole of Scotland Yard put together. He's outside now, keeping guard over the warders until we get you loose. . . . Curse these knots!
(*Meanwhile, the* 1ST J. *continues to count. But the* LUNATICS *are becoming less attentive. Those who are standing close to* ALAN *begin to take an interest in the* 2ND JOURNALIST'S *activities*)

LUNATIC What are you doing that for?

2ND J.   Can't you see? I'm tying him up tighter. The ropes had got loose. See this one? (*He holds it up*) It had slipped right off. (*He throws it away*) No good at all.
(*He continues to unfasten the other ropes and straps*)

LUNATIC   I'll help you.
(*Begins to refasten the straps*)

2ND J.   Don't bother, old boy. I can manage by myself.
(*Unfastens them again*)

LUNATIC   It's no bother. I like helping people. I'm a Boy Scout.

2ND J.   Well, do your day's good deed by leaving me alone, see?

LUNATIC   I don't think that would be a good deed, would it?

2ND J.   You bet it would!

LUNATIC   Perhaps you're right. But I'd better just ask the others what they think. (*In a very loud voice*) I say!
(*All the* LUNATICS *turn round to look at him*)

2ND J.   Holy Moses, that's torn it!

1ST LUNATIC   What are you doing with our prisoner?

2ND L.   Where's your warrant?

3RD L.   Habeas Corpus!

4TH L.   It's a rescue!

5TH L.   Stand by the doors!

OTHERS   Fire! Murder! Treason!
(*The* 1ST JOURNALIST, *now disregarded, rushes to the Leader's picture and gets behind it*)

1ST J. (*through the loud-speaker*)   Company! Fall in!
(*The* LUNATICS *immedIately form a double rank, facing the Leader's picture.* 2ND J. *continues feverishly with the work of untying* ALAN)

1ST J.   Slooope Hyppp!
(*The* LUNATICS *go through the motion of sloping arms*)

1ST J.   Oddah Hyppp!
(LUNATICS *order arms*)

1ST J.   Slooope Hyppp! (*They do so*) Oddah Hyppp! (*They do so*)

2ND J. (*to* ALAN)   That's all the drill he knows! (*Undoing*

the last strap) There! Come on, this is where we scoot!
(*They rush out*)

1ST J.   Company! Man the aeroplane! Fall out!
(*The* LUNATICS *rush to the structure of beds and scramble upon it. The* 1ST JOURNALIST *slips from behind the picture and runs out after the others*)

1ST LUNATIC   Start her up!
(*The* LUNATICS *imitate the roaring of the engines*)

1ST L.   Off we go! Faster! Faster! She's left the ground! We're rising! Higher! Higher!
(*The* LUNATICS *wave their handkerchiefs and grimace at the audience*)

A MAD LADY   Isn't the view gorgeous?

2ND MAD LADY   Look, there's the asylum. Just a tiny little speck!

A MAD LADY   I'll spit down the chimney!
(*Spits*)

THE PILOT   Hold on tight! I'm going to loop the loop!
(*Shrieks of dismay. The* LUNATICS *heave the beds up on end until the whole structure collapses. General confusion.* ALAN, *the* JOURNALISTS *and the* DOG *peep in for a moment at the window and disappear laughing*)

CURTAIN

Chorus

Paddington. King's Cross. Euston. Liverpool Street:
Each hiding behind a gothic hotel its gigantic greenhouse
And the long trains groomed before dawn departing at ten,
Picking their way through slums between the washing and the
　　　privies
To a clear run through open country,
Ignoring alike the cathedral towns in their wide feminine val-
　　　leys, and the lonely junctions.
In such a train sit Norman and his dog
Moving backwards through Westland at a mile a minute
And playing hearts with their two friends on an open mackin-
　　　tosh:

Picture the Pullman car with its deft attendants
And the usual passengers: the spoilt child, the corridor addict,
The lady who expects you to admire her ankles: the ostenta-
    tious peruser of important papers, etc. etc.
They have been travelling all day, it is late afternoon.
Outside the windows of the warm sealed tube, as a background
    to their conversation,
Imagine a hedgeless country, the source of streams;
Such as the driver, changing up at last, sees stretching from
    Hartside east and south,
Deadstones above Redan, Thackmoss, Halfpenny Scar,
Two Top and Muska, Pity Mea, Bullpot Brow:
Land of the ring ousel: a bird stone-haunting, an unquiet bird.

Scene II

(In a railway-train. ALAN, *the* TWO JOURNALISTS *and the* DOG
are playing cards. A little distance off sits the FINANCIER, *at
present half hidden by his newspaper)*

1ST J.   Your lead, Alan.
    (Alan plays. 1ST J. *plays a card)*

ALAN   *(to* 2ND J.*)*   Eight to beat.

2ND J.   *(looking at* DOG*)*   Hm . . . shall I risk it? No, I don't
think so.
    (He plays a card. The DOG *also plays a card)*

1ST J.   *(suspiciously)*   Hullo, you short-suited? Here, let's see
your hand.
    (He reaches out to take the DOG's *cards. The* DOG *growls and
refuses to show them)*

ALAN   Show them to me, Francis. Good Dog! (DOG *reluctantly
hands over the cards)* But you've got Slippery Anne here,
look!

2ND J.   Darned if he hasn't been cheating again.

ALAN   *(indignantly)*   He wasn't cheating! He just doesn't understand the rules, do you Doggy?

1ST J.   If you ask me, that Dog of yours understands a damn
sight too much. He's too smart by half. *(Yawns)* Well,
gentlemen, you've cleaned me out. I'll go and stretch myself

a bit. (*Standing up, he catches sight of the* FINANCIER: *sits down abruptly: to* 2ND J., *in a whisper*) Great God, man, look!

2ND J.   Where?

1ST J.   There!

2ND J.   Snakes! It isn't . . . ?

1ST J.   Bet you a fiver it is!

2ND J.   The papers say he's in Manchukuo.

1ST J.   Just eyewash!

2ND J.   Boy! I believe you're right!

ALAN (*loudly*)   What's all the fuss about!

1ST J.   Ssh!

2ND J.   Sssh!!

ALAN   You might tell a fellow!

1ST J. (*stage whisper*)   Grabstein! Sitting just behind you!

ALAN   Grabstein?

2ND J.   Ssh!

ALAN   Who's he when he's at home?

1ST J.   Oh boy, where were you educated? (*Wearily, to* 2ND J.) Go on, you tell him.

2ND J.   President of the X.Y.Z.

1ST J.   Chairman of the Pan-Asiatic.

2ND J.   Practically owns South America.

1ST J.   The biggest crook in Europe. Got his finger in everything. Whatever happens, he's in on the ground floor. Why, he even gets to hear of things before *we* do, sometimes!

ALAN   I say! Not really! I wonder if he knows where Francis is?

2ND J.   Most likely he does. The question is: would he tell you?

1ST J. (*winking at* 2ND J.)   Go and ask him.

ALAN   Shall I really?

2ND J. (*winking at* 1ST J.)   Atta boy!

ALAN (*doubtfully*)   All right. . . . If you don't think he'd mind?

1ST J.   Hell! Why should he?

2ND J.   He'll welcome you with open arms.

1ST J.   (*artfully*)   By the way, you might ask him a few other
questions while you're about it. Find out what holdings he
has in Sahara Electrics.

2ND J.   And how much it cost him to start the war in Spits-
bergen?

1ST J.   And what became of the Cloaguan Prime Minister
after the Platinum Scandals?

ALAN   I say, hold on a minute: I shall never remember all
that! Just give me time to write it down.
(*He takes a piece of paper from his pocket and makes notes.
The* JOURNALISTS *whisper instructions into his ear*)

ALAN   But won't he think me awfully inquisitive?

2ND J.   Oh, he loves being asked questions. . . . Just go up
to him and say: "Potts." That's the name of a very dear
friend of his. It'll put him in a good temper at once.

ALAN   (*doubtfully*)   Righto.
(*He approaches the* FINANCIER. *The* JOURNALISTS *shake
hands with each other in ecstasies of delight*)

1ST J.   Oh boy, I wouldn't have missed this for a thousand
pounds!
(*During the following scene, the* JOURNALISTS *take photographs and make notes*)

ALAN   (*rather nervously*)   Potts.
(*The* FINANCIER *looks up from his newspaper, stares at him
for a moment, turns deadly pale. Then, with a shrug of his
shoulders, he takes a cheque-book from his pocket and un-
screws the cap of his fountain-pen*)

FINANCIER   (*with a deep sigh*)   How much do you want?

ALAN   I beg your pardon, sir. I don't quite understand.

FINANCIER   (*more firmly*)   I'll give you a thousand: Not one
penny more. And you understand that I'm doing it because
I don't choose to be annoyed at this particular moment. I
have reasons for remaining incognito. I suppose you counted
on that? Very well . . . But let me warn you, if you're fool
enough to imagine that you can play this game twice, you
were never more mistaken. I have ways of dealing with
gentry of your sort. Understand?

ALAN   I'm awfully sorry, sir. But I think you must be making some mistake. . . . I only wanted to ask you a few questions. . . . It's frightful cheek of me, I know. . . .

FINANCIER   Oh, a journalist, eh? That's bad enough. Still, as you're here, I suppose I can let you have five minutes. Ask away. . . .

ALAN   (*consulting his notes*)   First of all, did you forge the report on the diamond mines on Tuesday Island?
(*The* FINANCIER *gasps*)

ALAN   (*continuing hurriedly*)   Secondly, is it true that you staged the fake attempt on the Prince of Hellespont in order to corner the rubber market?

FINANCIER   Do you seriously expect me to answer that?

ALAN   Well, no sir. To be quite candid, I don't. Please don't be angry. . . . Thirdly, did you have the men murdered who were going to show up the Bishop of Pluvium?

FINANCIER   (*laughs*)   Young man, you amuse me. Very well, since you're the first newspaper man who's ever dared to talk to me like this, I'll tell you the truth. The answer to all your three questions is: "Yes. I did." There! Now you've got a grand story, haven't you? Go and ask your editor to print it and he'll kick you out into the street. What's your paper, by the way? Ten to one, I own it.

ALAN   The Pressan Ambo Parish Magazine.

FINANCIER   Never heard of it. But I'll buy it tomorrow, lock, stock and barrel. How much would your boss take, do you suppose?

ALAN   I'm afraid I couldn't tell you that, sir. You see I only write for it occasionally. A bit of poetry now and then. Awful rot, I expect you'd think it.

FINANCIER   (*groans*)   Good God! Don't say you're a poet too!

ALAN   Oh rather not, sir!

FINANCIER   Glad to hear it. Of course, mind you, I've nothing against poets, provided they make good. They say that one or two fellows at the top of the tree are earning as much as four thousand a year. I doubt it myself. . . . But the fact remains that most of them are moral degenerates or Bolsheviks, or both. The scum of the earth. My son's a poet.

ALAN   I'm sorry, sir.

FINANCIER (*sentimentally*)   It's been the greatest disappoint-
ment of my whole life. Who have I got to work for, to be
proud of? Nobody. And my wife encourages him; the bitch.
As long as she's got her cocaine and her gigolos, we can all
go to hell as far as she's concerned. . . . I don't know why
I'm telling you all this.

ALAN (*politely*)   It's rotten luck for you, sir.

FINANCIER   Look here. I've taken a fancy to you. Will you be
my secretary? Starting at five thousand a year, with all
extras. Yes or no?

ALAN   It's most awfully kind of you, sir: but I'm afraid I
can't. . . .

FINANCIER (*emotionally*)   There, you see! I knew it! You
don't like me. None of them like me. Wherever I go I see it.
I can't so much as get a really friendly smile out of a railway-
porter, though Heaven knows I tip them enough. . . .
(*Sings. Accompaniment by dining-car attendant with gong*)
> When I was young I showed such application,
>   I worked the whole day long;
> I hoped to rise above my station,
>   To rise just like a song:
> I did so want to be a hero
>   In just a rich man's way
> But I might just as well be Nero,
>   And this is all I have to say:

CHORUS (*with* ATTENDANT *and* JOURNALISTS)
> Why are they so rude to me?
> It seems so crude to me,
> I want to be friendly
> But it's no good, for
> No one has love for me,
> Only a shove for me,
> They bait me and hate me, I'm
> Misunderstood.

FINANCIER
> I've founded hospitals and rest-homes,
>   Subscribed to public funds,
> Promoted schemes for planning Best Homes
>   And built a school for nuns.
> I've studied all the Italian Masters,
>   I've tried to read French books,

But all my efforts seem disasters:
I only get such nasty looks.

CHORUS
Why are they so rude to me, . . . etc.

FINANCIER Now what is it? Tell me straight out; don't be afraid. Is it my face? Is it my voice? Is it my manner? Or are you all just jealous of my damned money?

ALAN It isn't that, sir. Really it isn't. But you see . . . I'm not free. I've got a kind of job . . . if you can call it a job. . . .

FINANCIER Chuck it. I'll give you six thousand.

ALAN You see, sir, it's not that kind of job: that you can chuck up, I mean. . . . I've got to look for someone. He's Sir Francis Crewe, Bart. At least, he's Bart if he's alive. . . . That's what I really came to ask you about. . . . He ran away from home ten years ago. I thought you might happen to know where he is.

FINANCIER What do you take me for? A nursemaid?
(*The train stops. A* PORTER *looks in at the window*)

PORTER All change for Malago, Reykjavik and Omsk!

FINANCIER I must get out here. Will you take ten thousand? Yes or no? It's my last word.

ALAN I'm truly most terribly sorry, but. . . .

FINANCIER You're more of a fool than I took you for. (*Sentimentally*) Write to me sometimes and tell me how you're getting on. It would be so lovely to get a letter which had nothing to do with business!

ALAN Rather, sir!

FINANCIER Oh, by the way, a good place to look for that Baronet of yours would be Paradise Park. This train'll take you there. It's where most wasters and cranks land up sooner or later, if they've still got some cash to be swindled out of. You'll meet my dear son, among others. Perhaps you'll be able to knock some sense into him. Tell him I offer him a hundred thousand if he'll stop writing his drivel and clean a sewer. Goodbye.

ALAN Goodbye, sir. Thanks awfully.
(*The* FINANCIER, *with the help of* ALAN *and the* PORTER, *descends from the train*)

1ST J. (*to* 2ND J.)   Quick, we mustn't lose sight of him! If we follow him now, maybe we'll get the dope on that Dripping Merger, after all!
(*They leave the train*)

2ND J. (*to* ALAN)   You coming, Kid?

ALAN   I can't, I'm afraid. I've just got a new clue.

1ST J.   Well, good luck.

2ND J.   Ta ta.

ALAN   Goodbye, and thanks most awfully for all you've done.
(*The train moves on.* ALAN *waves from the window. Then he turns to the* DOG)

ALAN   Well, Doggy. We're all alone, now. Just you and me.
(*He puts his arm round the* DOG's *neck*) I wonder what Iris is doing? Oh dear, I wish we weren't such a long way from home. . . .
(*He gazes sadly out of the window*)

CURTAIN

Chorus

Happy the hare at morning, for she cannot read
The Hunter's waking thoughts. Lucky the leaf
Unable to predict the fall. Lucky indeed
The rampant suffering suffocating jelly
Burgeoning in pools, lapping the grits of the desert,
The elementary sensual cures,
The hibernations and the growth of hair assuage:
Or best of all the mineral stars disintegrating quietly into light.
But what shall men do, who can whistle tunes by heart,
Know to the bar when death shall cut him short, like the cry of
the shearwater?
We will show you what he has done.
How comely are his places of refuge and the tabernacles of his
peace,
The new books upon the morning table, the lawns and the
afternoon terraces!
Here are the playing-fields where he may forget his ignorance
To operate within a gentleman's agreement: twenty-two sins
have here a certain licence.

Here are the thickets where accosted lovers combatant
    May warm each other with their wicked hands,
Here are the avenues for incantation and workshops for the
    cunning engravers.
The galleries are full of music, the pianist is storming the keys,
    the great cellist is crucified over his instrument,
That none may hear the ejaculations of the sentinels
Nor the sigh of the most numerous and the most poor; the thud
    of their falling bodies
Who with their lives have banished hence the serpent and the
    faceless insect.

Scene III

(*The gardens of Paradise Park. A beautifully-kept lawn. Numbers of people are walking about the stage in sports clothes of various kinds or propelling themselves hither and thither in invalid chairs. Some lie on the grass absorbed in books. In the background are two large trees. In one of the trees sits the* POET, *smoking cigarettes: In the other are two* LOVERS *dressed in nursery-teapot-Dutch costumes. In the distance, the band plays a waltz*)

CHORUS   When you're in trouble,
        When you get the air,
    When everything returns your ring
        Do not despair, because although
    Friends may forsake you
        And all skies are dark
    You can be gay if you just step this way
        Into Paradise Park.

    Was it a tiring day
        On your office stool?
    Has your wife all your life
        Made you feel a fool? Don't cry, for though
    Landlords perplex you
        And all bosses frown,
    In Paradise Park you can feel a young spark
        And do them down!

(*Enter* ALAN *and the* DOG. *They approach the* POET'S *tree*)

ALAN (*to* POET)   Excuse me, sir. Is this Paradise Park?

POET   ἔστιν Θάλασσα, τίς δέ νιν κατασβέσαι.

ALAN   I beg your pardon?

POET   Nil nimium studeo, Caesar, tibi velle placere nec scire utrum sis albus aut ater homo.

ALAN   I'm awfully sorry, but I don't understand. Do you speak English?

POET   Nessum maggior dolore che ricordarsi del tempo felice.

ALAN   I know a little German, if that will do. . . . Entschuldigen Sie, bitte. Koennen Sie mir sagen, ob dies ist der Garten von Paradies?

POET   Dans l'an trentième de mon age. . . . (ALAN *begins to move off*) Oh well, if you insist on talking our filthy native language, I suppose I must. . . . Give me a cigarette. I've finished mine.

ALAN   I'm so sorry. . . . Of course. . . .
       Is the name Sir Francis Crewe
       Known by any chance to you?

POET   Did you like it?

ALAN   Er . . . ?

POET   I'm so glad you did! I wrote it!

ALAN   Wrote what?

POET   "Advances New," of course. Now tell me, which section did you like the best? *Mandrake* is the best technically, of course. But *Cinders* is more the real me, I think.

ALAN   I'm afraid you misunderstood me. I said Sir Francis Crewe. I've been looking for him.

POET   "Your chase had a beast in view."

ALAN   You know where he is?

POET   Well, of course.

ALAN   Where?

POET   (*tapping his forehead*)   Here. Everything's here. You're here. He's here. This park's here. This tree's here. If I shut my eyes they all disappear.

ALAN   And what happens if I shut *my* eyes? Do you disappear, too?

POET   (*crossly*)   No, of course not! I'm the only real person in the whole world.

ALAN   Well, suppose your tree was cut down? It wouldn't be there when you looked for it.

POET   Nonsense! The axe wouldn't exist unless I thought of it. The woodcutter wouldn't exist either.

ALAN   Isn't your Father the famous financier?

POET   I used to think so. But I got tired of that and forgot him. Give me another cigarette.
(As he leans down, the DOG *jumps up and bites his hand)*

POET   *(nursing his hand)*   Why can't you keep your blasted dog in order? Oh, my poor hand!

ALAN   I'm most dreadfully sorry. But you see, he's never seen a real person before. When you're only an imaginary dog and have been eating imaginary biscuits all your life, a real hand must taste simply delicious. You couldn't resist it, could you, Francis old boy? *(To* POET*)* Never mind. Just shut your eyes and you'll forget all about us.

POET   *(with his eyes shut)*   Oh, I've forgotten *you* long ago! It's my hand I keep remembering!
*(*ALAN *and* DOG *move on to the* LOVERS' *tree)*

1ST LOVER   Little white dove, it's you that I love,
           Fairer than hollyhocks far!
           How nice and how neat
           Are your dear little feet!
           You make my heart beat!
           How terribly sweet, how terribly sweet,
           How terribly sweet you are!
(They hug each other, taking no notice of ALAN*)*

ALAN   Excuse me, please, disturbing you:
       But have you heard of Sir Francis Crewe?

2ND L.   Have you, darling?

1ST L.   Oh, pretty starling!
         Say that again
         And again and again!
         I love to watch your cheek
         Move when you speak!

2ND L.   Oh dearest, you mustn't go on so!
         There's a nice man down below
         And there is something he wants to know.

1ST L.   Good morning. Let me introduce my wife.
         We're going to be lovers all our life:

RANSOM   You too. . . . Stagmantle's latest convert. He should be honoured.

SHAWCROSS   What's the point of all this talk? The people in England expect us to get to the top before the Ostnians. They believe in us. Are we going to let them down?

GUNN   I think this makes it all the more exciting. Good old Blavek!

RANSOM   Very well then, since you wish it. I obey you. The summit will be reached, the Ostnians defeated, the Empire saved. We have betrayed ourselves. We start at dawn.

CURTAIN

(*The Stage-Box on the right is illuminated. The* A*.'s are having breakfast*)

MRS. A.   Give me some money before you go,
There are a number of bills we owe
And you can go to the bank today
During the lunch-hour.

MR. A.   I dare say;
But, as it happens, I'm overdrawn.

MRS. A.   Overdrawn? What on earth have you done
With all the money? Where's it gone?

MR. A.   How does money always go?
Papers, lunches, tube-fares, teas,
Tooth-paste, stamps and doctor's fees,
Our trip to Hove cost a bit, you know.

MRS. A.   Can we never have fun? Can we never have any
And not have to count every single penny?
Why can't you find a way to earn more?
It's so degrading and dull to be poor.
Get another job.

MR. A.   My job may be small
But I'm damned lucky to have one at all.
When I think of those I knew in the War,
All the fellows about my age:
How many are earning a decent wage?
There was O'Shea, the middle-weight champion;
    slouches from bar to bar now in a battered hat,
    cadging for drinks;

There was Morgan, famous for his stories; sells
 ladies' underwear from door to door;
There was Polewhele, with his university education;
 now Dan the Lavatory Man at a third-rate
 night-club;
And Holmes in our office, well past fifty, was dismissed last week to bring down expenses;
Next week another: who shall it be?
It may be anyone. It may be me.

(*A newspaper is dropped through the door into the back
of the Box.* MR. A. *goes to fetch it*)

MRS. A. It's all this foreign competition:
 Czechoslovakia, Russia, Japan,
 Ostnia and Westland do all they can
 To ruin our trade with their cheap goods,
 Dumping them on our market in floods.
 It makes my blood boil! You can find
 No British goods of any kind
 In any of the big shops now.
 The Government ought to stop it somehow——

MR. A. Listen to this. (*Reads*) Our Special Correspondent
reports that the Ostnian Expedition to F 6, headed by
Blavek, has crossed the Tung Desert and is about to com-
mence its final assault on the mountain. Blavek is confident
of success and, in mountaineering circles, it is believed that
the British climbers will have to make very strenuous efforts
indeed if they are to beat their formidable opponents. . . .

MRS. A. You see? The foreigner everywhere,
 Competing in trade, competing in sport,
 Competing in science and abstract thought:
 And we just sit down and let them take
 The prizes! There's more than a mountain at stake.

MR. A. The travelogue showed us a Babylon buried in sand.

MRS. A. And books have spoken of a Spain that was the
 brilliant centre of an Empire.

MR. A. I have found a spider in the opulent boardroom.

MRS. A. I have dreamed of a threadbare barnstorming actor,
 and he was a national symbol.

MR. A. England's honour is covered with rust.

MRS. A. Ransom must beat them! He must! He must!

MR. A.   Or England falls. She has had her hour
And now must decline to a second-class power.
(*Puts on his bowler hat and exits, brandishing his news-
paper. The Stage-Box is darkened*)

Scene II

(*On F 6. At the foot of the West Buttress. The back of the
stage rises slightly, suggesting a precipice beyond. A magnificent panorama of distant mountains. On the right of the stage,
the wall of the buttress rises, with an overhang. Midday.* RAN-
SOM, SHAWCROSS *and* LAMP *stand roped on the edge of the
precipice, assisting the* DOCTOR *and* GUNN, *who are still out of
sight, below. The rope is belayed round a rock*)

RANSOM (*looking down*)   There's a hold to your left, Tom.
No, a little higher up. Good. Now you're all right.

GUNN'S VOICE (*from below*)   Look out, Doc. Don't tread on
my face!

RANSOM   Now then. . . . (*After a moment, the* DOCTOR
hoists himself into view, panting)   Now you take it easy,
Tom. Fifteen minutes' rest, here.

LAMP   We've made good time, this morning.

RANSOM (*looking down*)   You all right, David?

GUNN'S VOICE (*from below*)   I think so. . . . No! Ooh, er!
Gosh, this rock is soft! Here we come!
(*He appears*)

DOCTOR   Well, thank goodness, that couloir's behind us, anyhow. Though how we shall ever get down it again is another
matter.

RANSOM   You were splendid, Tom. Never known you in
better form.

DOCTOR   I must have lost at least two stone. That's one comfort.

GUNN   While we were in the chimney, I felt his sweat dripping
on to me like a shower-bath. . . . I say, isn't there anything more to eat?

RANSOM   I'm afraid we must keep to our rations, David. We're only carrying the minimum, you know.

SHAWCROSS   I should have thought you'd eaten enough to satisfy even *your* appetite—considering you had all my chocolate, as well.

GUNN   Well, you needn't make a grievance out of it. You didn't want it, did you?

DOCTOR   Still feeling sick, Ian?

SHAWCROSS (*crossly*)   I'm all right.

DOCTOR   You don't look any too good.

SHAWCROSS   Anyhow, I don't see that it helps much to keep fussing about trifles and thinking of one's comfort.
(*A pause*)

LAMP   Well, if we've got another ten minutes to spare, I think I'll be taking a look round. Might spot a clump of Polus Naufrangia. You never know. It's about the right altitude, now.
(*He goes to the back of the stage and looks over, through his binoculars*)

GUNN (*following him*)   See anything? (LAMP *shakes his head*) Gosh, that's a drop! (*He balances on the edge and pretends to wabble*) Ooh, er! Help!

RANSOM   Come away from there, David.
(GUNN *obeys and begins wandering about the stage*)

DOCTOR (*pointing upwards*)   How high do you make that buttress?

RANSOM   About seventeen hundred feet. We shall be on it all this afternoon. We ought to reach the ridge easily by sunset.

GUNN (*poking about*)   Hullo, what's this? (*Picks up a skull*) Doctor Livingstone, I presume? (*The others, except* LAMP, *who continues to peer through his binoculars, collect round* GUNN) How on earth did he get here?

DOCTOR   Goodness knows. May have fallen from above. See this crack? It's hardly likely to have been murder, up here.

SHAWCROSS   Anyhow, he must have been a pretty useful climber to have got as far as he did. I suppose there's no doubt it's a native skull?

DOCTOR   Impossible to say. It may have been some mad European who thought he'd have a shot at F 6 on his own; but that's scarcely possible. Some herdsman, probably. . . . What do you think, M. F.?
(*Hands him the skull*)

LAMP (*shouting excitedly*)   Come here! Look!

GUNN   What's the matter, Teddy?

LAMP   Polus Naufrangia! Five-leaved! A beauty! Only just spotted it. And it was right under my nose!
(*He begins lowering himself over the edge*)

DOCTOR   Wait a moment, Teddy. Better do that on the rope.

GUNN (*looking over*)   He'll be all right. It's a broad ledge. Only about twenty feet down.

DOCTOR (*looking over*)   Careful, Teddy. Careful. Take your time.

LAMP'S VOICE (*from below*)   I'm all right.
(*The others, except* RANSOM, *stand looking over the edge*)

RANSOM (*to skull*)   Well, Master; the novices are here. Have your dry bones no rustle of advice to give them? Or are you done with climbing? But that's improbable. Imagination sees the ranges in the Country of the Dead, where those to whom a mountain is a mother find an eternal playground. There Antoine de Ville scales pinnacles with subtle engines; Gesner drinks water, shares his dreams with Saussure, whose passion for Mont Blanc became a kind of illness. Paccard is reconciled with Balmont, and Bourrit, the cathedral precentor, no longer falsifies their story. Marie-Coutett still keeps his nickname of The Weasel; Donkin and Fox are talking of the Caucasus; Whymper goes climbing with his friends again and Hadow, who made the slip of inexperience, has no faults. While, on the strictest buttresses, the younger shadows look for fresher routes: Toni Schmidt is there and the Bavarian cyclists; and that pair also whom Odell saw on the step of Everest before the cloud hid them for ever, in the gigantic shadow of whose achievement we pitch our miserable tent——
(*The roar of an approaching avalanche is heard*)

DOCTOR   An avalanche! My God! (RANSOM *runs to join the others*) Look out, Teddy! Look out!

GUNN   Quick, man!

SHAWCROSS   Stay where you are!

GUNN   Jump for it!

DOCTOR   Oh, God! He's done for!
(*The roar of the avalanche drowns their voices; then gradually dies away*)

SHAWCROSS   He was just stooping to pick the flower, when the first stone got him.

DOCTOR   It was all over in a moment. He was probably knocked right out.

SHAWCROSS   As he went over the edge, you could see the flower in his hand.

GUNN   Gosh, I feel beastly!
(*Sits down on a rock*)

SHAWCROSS   He was a damn good man!

DOCTOR   I'm glad he found the Naufrangia, anyway. We must tell them that in London. Perhaps the five-leaved kind will be named after him. He'd like that, I think.

SHAWCROSS   I just can't believe it. Five minutes ago, he was standing here.

DOCTOR (*looking at* LAMP'S *rucksack, which is lying on a rock*)   What do you think we ought to do with this? His people might like to have it.

SHAWCROSS   We can't very well take it with us now. I think we'd better bury it here. We can pick it up on our way down.

DOCTOR   Right you are. I'll help you. (*Begins collecting stones*)
(SHAWCROSS *picks up the rucksack*)

GUNN   Poor old Teddy! (*To* SHAWCROSS) Half a minute! (*Feels in the pocket of the rucksack*) Oh, good!
(*Pulls out a piece of chocolate and begins eating it*)

SHAWCROSS (*horrified*)   My God! Haven't you any decency left in you at all?

GUNN (*with his mouth full*)   Why, what's the matter now?

SHAWCROSS   Of all the filthy callousness!

GUNN   But, honestly, I don't see anything wrong. He doesn't want it now, does he?

SHAWCROSS If that's the line you take, I suppose there's no
more to be said. . . . Get some stones!
(*While the others are burying the rucksack,* RANSOM *stoops
and picks up* LAMP'S *snowglasses, which he has left lying on
the rocks at the back of the stage*)

RANSOM The first victim to my pride. If I had never asked
him, he would not have come. The Abbot was perfectly
right. My minor place in history is with the aberrant group
of Caesars: the dullard murderers who hale the gentle from
their beds of love and, with a quacking drum, escort them
to the drowning ditch and the death in the desert. . . . (*To
the others*) You have forgotten these. (*Gives glasses*)
Hurry up. We must be getting on. Ian, will you change
places with David?
(*Music. They rope up in silence.* RANSOM *begins the traverse
round the buttress, as the* CURTAIN *slowly falls*)

(*Both Stage-Boxes are illuminated. In the left-hand box,* STAG-
MANTLE *is at the microphone. In the right-hand box, the* A.'s
sit, listening. MR. A. *is playing Patience.* MRS. A. *is darning
socks*)

STAGMANTLE It is with the deepest regret that we have to
announce the death of Mr. Edward Lamp, a member of
the F 6 Expedition. He was climbing along a ridge on the
north face after a rare botanical specimen when he was
caught by an avalanche and killed. He was twenty-four
years of age.

In Edward Lamp, Science has lost one of her most brilliant recruits. At Cambridge he carried everything before
him; and his career, so tragically cut short, promised to be
of the highest distinction. He died as he had lived: in the
service of his austere mistress. This is as he would have
wished; and no man can do more. Nor could one design
him a more fitting grave than among the alpine flowers he
loved so passionately and with such understanding. . . .
(*Exit*)

MRS. A.   (*moved*)
            Death like his is right and splendid;
            That is how life should be ended!
            He cannot calculate nor dread
            The mortifying in the bed,
            Powers wasting day by day
            While the courage ebbs away.

Ever-charming, he will miss
The insulting paralysis,
Ruined intellect's confusion,
Ulcer's patient persecution,
Sciatica's intolerance
And the cancer's sly advance;
Never hear, among the dead,
The rival's brilliant paper read,
Colleague's deprecating cough
And the praises falling off;
Never know how in the best
Passion loses interest;
Beauty sliding from the bone
Leaves the rigid skeleton.

MR. A. If you had seen a dead man, you would not
Think it so beautiful to lie and rot;
I've watched men writhing on the dug-out floor
Cursing the land for which they went to war;
The joker cut off halfway through his story,
The coward blown involuntary to glory,
The steel butt smashing at the eyes that beg,
The stupid clutching at the shattered leg,
The twitching scarecrows on the rusty wire;
I've smelt Adonis stinking in the mire,
The puddle stolid round his golden curls,
Far from his precious mater and the girls;
I've heard the gas-case gargle, green as grass,
And in the guns, Death's lasting animus.
Do you think it would comfort Lamp to know
The British Public mourns him so?
I tell you, he'd give his rarest flower
Merely to breathe for one more hour!
What is this expedition? He has died
To satisfy our smug suburban pride. . . .

  (*The Stage-Boxes are darkened*)

Scene III

(*On F 6.* CAMP A. *The left of stage is occupied by a tent, which
is open at the end facing the audience. Behind it, to the right,
the ground rises to a platform of rock, over-hanging a precipice. It is early evening: during the dialogue which follows, the*

stage slowly darkens. Wind noises. RANSOM *and the* DOCTOR *are inside the tent, preparing a meal. The* DOCTOR *is cooking on the Primus stove*)

DOCTOR   The wind's getting up again. It's going to be a bad night. . . . I wish those two would turn up.

RANSOM   We can't expect them just yet. They're loaded, remember; and the going isn't easy.

DOCTOR   What was the psychrometer reading?

RANSOM   6.5.

DOCTOR   We're in for a lot more snow.

RANSOM   It looks like it.

DOCTOR   And if it's bad down here, what's it going to be like up there on the arrête?

RANSOM   (*smiling*)   Worse.

DOCTOR   M. F.—you can't start to-morrow!

RANSOM   I must.

DOCTOR   If you try it in this weather, you haven't a chance!

RANSOM   We shall have a better chance to-morrow than the day after. Three days from now, there'd be none at all. We can't hang on here for more than four days: we haven't the stores.

DOCTOR   To try the arrête in a blizzard is sheer madness!

RANSOM   Hasn't this whole climb been madness, Tom? We've done things in the last week which ought to have been planned and prepared for months. We've scrambled up here somehow, and now we must make a rush for it. . . . Whatever the weather is, I must leave for the summit to-morrow.

DOCTOR   Very well, M. F. You didn't bring me up here to argue with you. I won't. Just tell me what you want me to do.

RANSOM   To-day is Tuesday. You'll wait for us here till Friday, at dawn. If we aren't back by then, you'll descend at once to Camp B, rest there as long as necessary and then carry out the evacuation of the mountain, as we arranged. . . . You understand, Tom? At once. There is to be no delay of any kind.

DOCTOR   You mean: no search party?

RANSOM   Nothing. If you like, I'll put that in writing. I forbid all useless risks. (*Smiling*) I order you to return to England alive.

DOCTOR   (*smiling*)   You'd better repeat that order to David personally.

RANSOM   It won't be necessary.

DOCTOR   What do you mean?

RANSOM   David is coming with me to the summit.

DOCTOR   And Ian?

RANSOM   He'll remain with you here.

DOCTOR   (*after a long pause*)   I don't like it, M. F.

RANSOM   Why not, Tom?

DOCTOR   I suppose you know best; but——

RANSOM   Don't imagine I haven't thought this over carefully. I know what you are going to say: Ian is steady, reliable, a first-class climber: David is only a brilliant amateur, a novice with an extraordinary flair, unsound, uneven, liable to moments of panic, without staying power. Yes, it's all true.

DOCTOR   Ian's wanted to do this climb with you more than he's ever wanted to do anything in his whole life.

RANSOM   I know. I've felt that, often. All these weeks, he's been on edge, straining every muscle and every nerve, never relaxing, torturing himself, denying himself, watching me like a dog waiting for a sign. . . . Already he's utterly exhausted; he's a feverish invalid. Take this sickness of his: as long as I've known him, Ian's never been sick on a mountain before. . . . You see, Tom, the ascent of F 6 represents, for Ian, a kind of triumph which he not only desires but of which he's desperately afraid. He can't face it. He wants me to order him to face it. But if I do, it will destroy him.

DOCTOR   (*after a pause*)   Perhaps you're right, M. F. . . . Yes, I think you are. But surely—you've admitted it yourself—David is afraid, too?

RANSOM   David is afraid of precipices, avalanches, cornices, falling stones. He is afraid of being killed; not of dying. He is not afraid of F 6, nor of himself.

DOCTOR M. F.—the boys have their whole lives before them. Take me.

RANSOM (*after a pause*) Yes, I'd thought of that, too. Thank you for asking me, Tom. I am very honoured.

DOCTOR Oh, I know it's impossible, of course. I'm a fat old man. The crystal was right: I shall die in my bed.

RANSOM You will die at the end of a long and useful life. You will have helped a great many people and comforted all whom you could not help. . . . But the Demon demands another kind of victim——
(*Whistling from* GUNN, *off. Enter* GUNN *and* SHAWCROSS, *R. Both of them are carrying stores. They cross the stage and enter the tent*)

GUNN Hullo, M. F.! Hullo, Doc.! Are we late for supper?

DOCTOR No, it's just ready now.
(GUNN *and* SHAWCROSS *put down their loads.* SHAWCROSS *is much exhausted:* GUNN *fresh and lively.* RANSOM *lights the tent lantern*)

GUNN Gosh, I'm hungry! The altitude doesn't seem to affect *my* appetite. What is there to eat?

DOCTOR Cocoa and oatmeal. (*Hands round rations*)

GUNN Oatmeal again!

DOCTOR Perhaps you'd prefer a mutton chop?

GUNN Don't, Tom, you swine! You make my mouth water! The first thing I'll do when I get back, I'll stand you dinner at Boulestin's. We'll start with two dozen Royal Whitstables——

DOCTOR Oh, but David, Danish are much better!

GUNN Just as you like. What about soup? Minestrone, I think?

DOCTOR You have that. I prefer a really good tomato to anything.

GUNN And now, what would you say to Lobster Newberg?

DOCTOR I oughtn't to, really; but I can't resist.

GUNN Good Lord! We've forgotten the wine!

SHAWCROSS (*bitterly*) Must you always be talking about food?

GUNN Was I? Sorry.

SHAWCROSS   Well, for God's sake, shut up then!
(*A pause*)

DOCTOR   You're not eating anything, Ian.

SHAWCROSS   I don't want any, thanks.

DOCTOR   Take just a little. You must eat something, you know.

SHAWCROSS   (*angrily*)   You heard me say No once. Are you going deaf?

RANSOM   Doctor's orders, Ian.

SHAWCROSS   All right, M. F. If you say so——

RANSOM   (*handing him his mug of cocoa*)   Try this. It's good.
(SHAWCROSS *sips listlessly, putting the mug down almost at once*)

GUNN   Thank God for my good dinner! Please may I get down? (*Pretending to strum on mandolin, sings:*)
> Some have tennis-elbow
> And some have housemaid's knee,
> And some I know have got B.O.:
> But these are not for me.
> There's love the whole world over
> Wherever you may be;
> I had an aunt who loved a plant—
> But you're my cup of tea!

DOCTOR   (*laughing and applauding*)   Bravo! (GUNN *bows*)
You know, M. F., this reminds me of our first climb together, on the Meije. Do you remember that hut?

RANSOM   And our Primus that wouldn't light? Shall I ever forget it?

DOCTOR   And the fleas in the straw? Extraordinary the altitudes fleas can live at! Funny things, fleas. . . . If a flea were as big as a man, it could jump over St. Paul's.

GUNN   When I was at school, I tried to keep a flea circus. But I could never train them to do anything at all. They're not really very intelligent.

DOCTOR   Perhaps you didn't go the right way about it. A man told me once that if——

SHAWCROSS   (*passionately*)   Oh, for Christ's sake, shut up!

DOCTOR   Why, what's the matter, Ian?

SHAWCROSS   Do you expect me to sit listening to your drivel the whole night? Why do we keep pretending like this? Why don't we talk of what we're all thinking about? M. F., I've had about as much of this as I can stand! You've got to tell us now: which of us are you taking with you to-morrow?

DOCTOR   Steady, Ian! (*Puts a hand on his arm*)

SHAWCROSS   (*shaking him off*)   Let me alone, damn you! I wasn't talking to you! M. F., you've bloody well got to choose!

RANSOM   I have chosen, Ian. I'm taking David.

SHAWCROSS   Oh, my God! (*Pause*) And I knew it all the time!

GUNN   Rotten luck, Ian. . . . I say, let me stay behind. . . . I don't mind, so very much. . . .

SHAWCROSS   (*shouting*)   My God, do you think I'm going to crawl for favours to *you,* you little swine! You were always his favourite! I don't know how I've kept my hands off you so long! (*He tries to throttle* GUNN: *the* DOCTOR *seizes him*)

DOCTOR   Ian, that's enough!

SHAWCROSS   (*struggling free*)   Oh, I know—you're on his side, too! Do you think I haven't heard you whispering behind my back?

RANSOM   Is this what all your talk of loyalty amounts to, Ian? Tom and David have nothing to do with this. I am in charge of this expedition. If you have anything to complain of, be man enough to say so to me.

SHAWCROSS   I'm sorry, M. F. Forgive me. You're quite right. I'm no damn good: I realize that now. You're all better men than I am. I had a pretty fine opinion of myself, once. I imagined I was indispensable. Even my admiration of you was only another kind of conceit. You were just an ideal of myself. But F 6 has broken me; it's shown me what I am —a rotten weakling. . . . I'll never give orders to anybody again.

RANSOM   No, Ian. You're wrong. F 6 hasn't broken you. It has made a man of you. You know yourself now. Go back to England with Tom. One day you will do something better worth while than this fool's errand on which David and I are going. I am giving you a harder job than mine.

SHAWCROSS (*hesitating*)   If I only could———! But you don't really believe it: I see you don't! No one will ever——— (*With rising excitement*) They'd look at me and think——— No, I couldn't bear it! He failed—I can't—no, no———I'll never let them! Never!
(*He turns to rush out of the tent*)

DOCTOR   Ian! (*They struggle at the tent flap;* SHAWCROSS *breaks free and runs across to the rock above the precipice; the others following*)

RANSOM   Stop him!

GUNN   Ian, you fool, come back!
(SHAWCROSS, *with a loud cry, springs over the precipice. The others reach the rock and stand peering down into the darkness. Gale noises and music*)

CURTAIN

(*Both Stage-Boxes are illuminated. In the right-hand Box, the* A.'s *are listening.* MRS. A. *is adjusting the wireless:* MR. A. *stands restlessly cleaning his pipe. In the left-hand Box, the* AN-NOUNCER *is at the microphone*)

ANNOUNCER   There is still no news of the British Expedition to F 6. Fort George reports that a severe blizzard is general over the whole range. The gravest anxiety is felt as to their safety———

MR. A.   Turn off the wireless; we are tired of descriptions of
                 travel;
              We are bored by the exploits of amazing heroes;
              We do not wish to be heroes, nor are we likely to
                 travel.
              We shall not penetrate the Arctic Circle
              And see the Northern Lights flashing far beyond
                 Iceland;
              We shall not hear the prayer from the minaret echo-
                 ing over Arabia
              Nor the surf on the coral atoll.

MRS. A.   Nor do we hope to be very distinguished;
              The embossed card of invitation is not for us;
              No photographers lurk at our door;
              The house-party and the grouse-moor we know by
                 hearsay only;

We know of all these from the lending library and
the super cinema.

MR. A.   They excite us; but not very much. It is not our life.

MRS. A.   For the skidding car and the neighbours' gossip
Are more terrifying to us than the snarling leap of
the tiger;
And the shop-fronts at Christmas a greater marvel
than Greece.

MR. A.   Let our fears and our achievements be sufficient to
our day.

MRS. A.   The luck at the bargain counter:

MR. A.   The giant marrow
grown on the allotment.

MRS. A.   Our moments of exaltation have not been extraordinary
But they have been real.

MR. A.   In the sea-side hotel, we experienced genuine passion:

MRS. A.   Straying from the charabanc, under tremendous
beeches,
We were amazed at the profusion of bluebells and
the nameless birds;
And the Ghost Train and the switchback did not
always disappoint.

MR. A.   Turn off the wireless. Tune in another station;
To the tricks of variety or the rhythm of jazz.
Let us roll back the carpet from the parlour floor
And dance to the wireless through the open door.

(*They turn on the wireless and a dance band is heard. The*
A.'*s leave the box*)

ANNOUNCER (*sings*)
Forget the Dead, what you've read,
All the errors and the terrors of the bed;
Dance, John, dance!
Ignore the Law, it's a bore,
Don't enumer all the rumours of a war;
Dance, John, dance!
Chin up!
Kiss me!
Atta Boy!
Dance till dawn among the ruins of a burning Troy!

Forget the Boss when he's cross,
All the bills and all the ills that make you toss:
Dance, John, dance!
Some get disease, others freeze,
Some have learned the way to turn themselves to trees;
Dance, John, etc.
(*The Stage-Boxes are darkened*)

Scene IV

(*On F 6. The Arrête. Hurricane. Late afternoon.* RANSOM *supporting* GUNN)

RANSOM   Steady. Lean on me.

GUNN   No, it's no use. I can't go any further. Help me down there, out of this bloody blizzard. (*They descend to a ledge . . . Collapsing*) Thanks. But hurry. Go on, now, and reach the top. F 6 is a household word already. The nursemaids in the park go into raptures. The barber's chatter's full of nothing else. You mustn't disappoint them. In London now, they are unlocking the entrances to tubes. I should be still asleep but not alone. Toni was nice but very difficult. . . . Now no policeman will summons me again for careless driving. . . . They're flagging from the pits. . . . I cannot stop. . . . The brakes are gone. . . . Ian would be feeling as sick as a cat. . . . Where is that brake? Two hundred. . . . Christ, what banking! (*Dies*)

RANSOM

You always had good luck; it has not failed you
Even in this, your brightest escapade,
But extricates you now
From the most cruel cunning trap of all,
Sets you at large and leaves no trace behind,
Except this dummy.
          O senseless hurricanes,
That waste yourselves upon the unvexed rock,
Find some employment proper to your powers,
Press on the neck of Man your murdering thumbs
And earn real gratitude! Astrologers,
Can you not scold the fated loitering star
To run to its collision and our end?
The Church and Chapel can agree in this,

The vagrant and the widow mumble for it
And those with millions belch their heavy prayers
To take away this luggage. Let the ape buy it
Or the insipid hen. Is Death so busy
That we must fidget in a draughty world
That's stale and tasteless; must we still kick our heels
And wait for his obsequious secretaries
To page Mankind at last and lead him
To the distinguished Presence?

CURTAIN

(The Stage-Boxes remain darkened. A voice from each is heard, in duet. They are like people speaking in their sleep)

LEFT BOX	RIGHT BOX
No news	
	Useless to wait
Too late	
	Their fate
	We do not know
Snow on the pass	
	Alas
Nothing to report	
	Caught in the blizzard
Fought through the storm	
	Warm in our beds we wonder
Thunder and hail	
	Will they fail? Will they miss their success?
Yes. They will die	
	We sigh. We cannot aid
They fade from our mind	
	They find no breath
But Death	

Scene V

(F 6. The stage rises steeply, in a series of rock terraces, to the small platform at the back which forms the summit of the mountain. Blizzard. Gathering darkness. In the front of the stage RANSOM *is struggling upwards. After a few numbed*

*movements, he falls exhausted. Music throughout. The light
now fades into complete darkness. The voices of the* CHORUS,
*dressed in the habit of the monks from the glacier monastery,
are heard*)

CHORUS

Let the eye of the traveller consider this country and weep,
For toads croak in the cisterns; the aqueducts choke with
leaves:
The highways are out of repair and infested with thieves:
The ragged population are crazy for lack of sleep:
Our chimneys are smokeless; the implements rust in the
field
And our tall constructions are felled.
Over our empty playgrounds the wet winds sough;
The crab and the sandhopper possess our abandoned
beaches;
Upon our gardens the dock and the darnel encroaches;
The crumbling lighthouse is circled with moss like a muff;
The weasel inhabits the courts and the sacred places;
Despair is in our faces.
(*The summit of the mountain is illuminated, revealing a
veiled seated figure*)
For the Dragon has wasted the forest and set fire to the
farm;
He has mutilated our sons in his terrible rages
And our daughters he has stolen to be victims of his disso-
lute orgies;
He has cracked the skulls of our children in the crook of
his arm;
With the blast of his nostrils he scatters death through the
land;
We are babes in his hairy hand.
O, when shall the deliverer come to destroy this dragon?
For it is stated in the prophecies that such a one shall ap-
pear,
Shall ride on a white horse and pierce his heart with a
spear;
Our elders shall welcome him home with trumpet and
organ,
Load him with treasure, yes, and our most beautiful maid-
enhead
He shall have for his bed.
(*The veiled figure on the summit raises its hand. There is
a fanfare of trumpets. The Dragon, in the form of* JAMES

RANSOM, *appears. He wears full ceremonial dress, with orders. He is illuminated by a spotlight. The* CHORUS, *throughout the whole scene, remain in semi-darkness. As* JAMES *appears the* CHORUS *utter a cry of dismay.* JAMES *bows to the* FIGURE)

JAMES   I am sorry to say that our civilising mission has been subject to grave misinterpretations. Our critics have been unhelpful, and, I am constrained to add, unfair. The powers which I represent stand unequivocally for peace. We have declared our willingness to conclude pacts of non-aggression with all of you—on condition, of course, that our demands are reasonably met. During the past few years we have carried unilateral disarmament to the utmost limits of safety; others, whom I need not specify, have unfortunately failed to follow our example. We now find ourselves in a position of inferiority which is intolerable to the honour and interests of a great power; and in self-defence we are reluctantly obliged to take the necessary measures to rectify the situation. We have constantly reiterated our earnest desire for peace; but in the face of unprovoked aggression I must utter a solemn warning to you all that we are prepared to defend ourselves to the fullest extent of our forces against all comers.

(JAMES *is seated*)

(*Duet from the darkened Stage-Boxes*)

DUET   Him who comes to set us free
          Save whoever it may be,
          From the fountain's thirsty snare,
          From the music in the air,
          From the tempting fit of slumber,
          From the odd unlucky number,
          From the riddle's easy trap,
          From the ignorance of the map,
          From the locked forbidden room,
          From the Guardian of the Tomb,
          From the siren's wrecking call,
          Save him now and save us all.

(*Flourish on the wood-wind.* MICHAEL RANSOM *steps into the light which surrounds the Dragon* JAMES. *He still wears his climbing things, but is without helmet, goggles or ice-axe*)

JAMES   Michael! Why have you come here? What do you want?

RANSOM   Hardly very friendly, are you?

JAMES   What is it this time? We are grown men now.

RANSOM   There is no time to lose. I have come to make you a most important proposition.

JAMES   Which I accept—on my own conditions. (*At his signal a complete set of life-size chessmen appear. The chief pieces on* JAMES' *side are* STAGMANTLE, ISABEL *and the* GENERAL; *and on* MICHAEL'S, SHAWCROSS, GUNN *and* LAMP. *All have masks which partially disguise them*) Before we continue, if any of you have any questions you would like to put either to my colleagues or myself, we shall be delighted to do our best to answer them.

(*As each character answers his question, he or she removes the mask*)

MR. A. (*from Stage-Box*)   Why is my work so dull?

GENERAL   That is a most insubordinate remark. Every man has his job in life, and all he has to think about is doing it as well as it can be done. What is needed is loyalty, not criticism. Think of those climbers up on F 6. No decent food. No fires. No nice warm beds. Do you think *they* grumble? You ought to be ashamed of yourself.

MRS. A.   Why doesn't my husband love me any more?

ISABEL   My dear, I'm terribly sorry for you. I do understand. But aren't you being just a teeny-weeny bit morbid? Now think of those young climbers up there on F 6. They're not worrying about their love affairs. (*Archly*) And I'm sure they must have several. Of course, I know people like you and me can't do big things like that, but we can find little simple everyday things which help to take us out of ourselves. Try to learn Bridge or get a book from the lending library. Reorganise your life. I know it won't be easy at first, but I'm sure if you stick to it you'll find you won't brood so much. And you'll be ever so much happier.

MR. A.   Why have I so little money?

STAGMANTLE   Ah, I was expecting that one! I'm a practical man like yourself, and as it happens I'm a rich one, so I ought to know something about money. I know there are far too many people who have too little. It's a damned shame, but there it is. That's the world we live in. But speaking quite seriously as a business man, I can tell you that money doesn't necessarily bring happiness. In fact, the

more you worry about it, the unhappier you are. The finest
and happiest man I ever met—he's leading the expedition
up F 6 at the moment—doesn't care a brass button for
money, and never has. So my advice is: Get all the cash
you can and stick to it, but don't worry.

MR. A.
        &   Why were we born?
MRS. A.

JAMES   That's a very interesting question, and I'm not sure
I can answer it myself. But I know what my brother, the
climber, thinks. When we take, he said to me once, the life
of the individual, with its tiny circumscribed area in space
and time, and measure it against the geological epochs, the
gigantic movements of history and the immensity of the
universe, we are forced, I think, to the conclusion that,
taking the large view, the life of the individual has no real
existence or importance apart from the great whole; that
he is here indeed but to serve for his brief moment his community, his race, his planet, his universe; and then, passing
on the torch of life undiminished to others, his little task
accomplished, to die and be forgotten.

RANSOM   You're not being fair to me.

JAMES   Keep to your world. I will keep to mine.
(*The chess game begins. Complete silence, accompanied
only by a drum roll. At intervals* JAMES *or* MICHAEL *says:*
"*Check!*")

JAMES   Check!

RANSOM (*looking for the first time towards the summit and
seeing the figure*) Look!

JAMES   Mate! I've won!
(*The* FIGURE *shakes its head*)

RANSOM (*his eyes still fixed upon it*)   But was the victory
real?

JAMES (*half rises to his feet, totters: in a choking voice*)   It
was not Virtue—it was not Knowledge—it was Power!
(*Collapses*)

CHORUS   What have you done? What have you done? You
have killed, you have murdered her favourite son!
(*Confusion. During the following speeches,* STAGMANTLE,
the GENERAL *and* ISABEL *jostle each other, jump on each*

other's shoulders to get a better hearing and behave in general like the Marx brothers)

STAGMANTLE   The whole of England is plunged into mourning for one of her greatest sons; but it is a sorrow tempered with pride, that once again Englishmen have been weighed in the balance and not found wanting.

ISABEL   At this hour, the thoughts of the whole nation go out to a very brave and very lonely woman in a little South Country cottage; already a widow and now a bereaved mother.

GENERAL   I am no climber; but I know courage when I see it. He was a brave man and courage is the greatest quality a man can have.

STAGMANTLE   Sport transcends all national barriers, and it is some comfort to realise that this tragedy has brought two great nations closer together.

ISABEL   In the face of this terrible tragedy, one is almost tempted to believe in the grim old legend of the Demon.
(*A figure having the shape of the* ABBOT, *wearing a monk's habit and a judge's wig and holding the crystal in his hands, is illuminated at a somewhat higher level of the stage*)

ABBOT   I am truly sorry for this young man, but I must ask for the Court to be cleared.
(*Exeunt* SHAWCROSS, LAMP *and* GUNN)
(*A Blues.* MONKS *enter with a stretcher.* JAMES' *body is carried in slow procession round the stage and away into the darkness*)

STAGMANTLE & ISABEL
Stop all the clocks, cut off the telephone,
Prevent the dog from barking with a juicy bone,
Silence the pianos and with muffled drum
Bring out the coffin, let the mourners come.

Let aeroplanes circle moaning overhead
Scribbling on the sky the message: He is dead.
Put crepe bows round the white necks of the public doves,
Let the traffic policemen wear black cotton gloves.

Hold up your umbrellas to keep off the rain
From Doctor Williams while he opens a vein;
Life, he pronounces, it is finally extinct.
Sergeant, arrest that man who said he winked!

Shawcross will say a few words sad and kind
To the weeping crowds about the Master-Mind,
While Lamp with a powerful microscope
Searches their faces for a sign of hope.

And Gunn, of course, will drive the motor-hearse:
None could drive it better, most would drive it worse.
He'll open up the throttle to its fullest power
And drive him to the grave at ninety miles an hour.

ABBOT   Please be seated, Mr. Ransom. I hope everything has
been arranged here to your satisfaction?

RANSOM   I didn't do it! I swear I didn't touch him! It wasn't
my fault. (*Pointing to* FIGURE) The Demon gave the sign!
The Demon is real!

ABBOT   In that case, we will call the victims of his pride. Call
Ian Shawcross.

CHORUS   Ian Shawcross!
(SHAWCROSS *appears. He is bloodstained and pale*)

RANSOM   I've had about as much of this as I can stand.
You've got to tell them. I hate to bother you with this sort
of thing.

SHAWCROSS   I'm afraid you haven't succeeded very well.

RANSOM   You mean, you *did* see something? If you hadn't,
you mightn't believe me.

SHAWCROSS   Oh, for Christ's sake, shut up! If what you've
done amuses you, I'm glad. I'm not very tolerant, I'm afraid.
(*Exit*)

ABBOT   Call David Gunn.

CHORUS   David Gunn!
(*Enter* DAVID GUNN, *pale and covered with snow. His face
is entirely without features*)

RANSOM   David, you saw what happened?

GUNN   Didn't I just? You did it beautifully. It was first class!

RANSOM   You sound pleased!

GUNN   Of course I'm pleased. Who wouldn't be!

RANSOM   David, there's something I *must* tell you——
(*Exit* GUNN)

ABBOT   Call Edward Lamp.

CHORUS   Edward Lamp! Edward Lamp! Edward Lamp!

LAMP'S VOICE (*far away, off*)   I'm all right.

RANSOM (*shouts*)   Teddy, what did you see?

LAMP'S VOICE   If I told you, you wouldn't be any the wiser.

RANSOM   You're on their side, too! Is this all your talk of loyalty amounts to?

MRS. A.   O, what's the use of your pretending
As if Life had a chance of mending?
There will be nothing to remember
But the fortnight in August or early September.

MR. A.   Home to supper and to bed.
It'll be like this till we are dead.
(DOCTOR *appears*)

RANSOM   Tom!

DOCTOR   Just tell me what you want me to do.

RANSOM   I can't face it!

DOCTOR   Perhaps you are right. The Demon demands another kind of victim. Ask the crystal.
(*Exit* DOCTOR)

ABBOT   You wish to appeal to the crystal, Mr. Ransom? Do not ask at once, but think it over.

RANSOM   We haven't a moment to lose. I appeal to the crystal.

ABBOT   Very well, since you wish it, I obey you. (*Looks into crystal*)
(MUSIC. DUET *from Stage-Boxes, the* A.'s *sing*)

MRS. A. & MR. A.   Make us kind,
Make us of one mind,
Make us brave,
Save, save, save, save.

ABBOT   Mr. Ransom, I did you an injustice. I thought I understood your temptation, but I was wrong. The temptation is not the Demon. If there were no Demon there would be no temptation.

RANSOM   What have I said? I didn't mean it! Forgive me! It was all my fault. F 6 has shown me what I am. I'm a coward and a prig. I withdraw the charge.

ABBOT   Such altruism, Mr. Ransom, is uncommon in one of your race. But I'm afraid it is too late now. The case is being brought by the Crown. (*Turning to the* FIGURE *on the summit*) Have you anything to say in your defence? (*Pause*) You realise the consequences of silence? (*Pause*) As long as the world endures there must be law and order. (*To* CHORUS) Gentlemen, consider your verdict.

CHORUS

At last the secret is out, as it always must come in the end,
The delicious story is ripe to tell to the intimate friend;
Over the tea-cups and in the square the tongue has its desire;
Still waters run deep, my dear, there's never smoke without fire.

Behind the corpse in the reservoir, behind the ghost on the links,
Behind the lady who dances and the man who madly drinks,
Under the look of fatigue, the attack of migraine and the sigh
There is always another story, there is more than meets the eye.

For the clear voice suddenly singing, high up in the convent wall,
The scent of the elder bushes, the sporting prints in the hall,
The croquet matches in summer, the handshake, the cough, the kiss,
There is always a wicked secret, a private reason for this.

ABBOT   Have you considered your verdict?

RANSOM   Stop!
(*He rushes up to the summit and places himself in front of the* FIGURE, *with his arms outstretched, as if to protect it*)

RANSOM   No one shall ever——! I couldn't bear it! I'll never let them! Never!

ABBOT (*to* CHORUS)   Guilty or not guilty?

CHORUS (*all pointing to the* FIGURE)   Guilty!

GENERAL   Die for England!

ISABEL   Honour!

STAGMANTLE   Service!

GENERAL   Duty!

ISABEL   Sacrifice!

ALL   Die for England, England, England!

MRS. A. & MR. A.   Die for us!
(*Thunder and the roar of an avalanche are heard. All lights
are extinguished below; only the* FIGURE *and* RANSOM *remain
illuminated.* RANSOM *turns to the* FIGURE, *whose draperies
fall away, revealing* MRS. RANSOM *as a young mother*)

RANSOM   Mother!

MOTHER (*Mrs. Ransom*)   My boy! At last!
(*He falls at her feet with his head in her lap. She strokes his
hair*)

CHORUS   Acts of injustice done
   Between the setting and the rising sun
   In history lie like bones, each one.

MRS. RANSOM   Still the dark forest, quiet the deep,
     Softly the clock ticks, baby must sleep!
     The Pole star is shining, bright the Great Bear,
     Orion is watching, high up in the air.

CHORUS   Memory sees them down there,
  Paces alive beside his fear
  That's slow to die and still here.

MRS. RANSOM   Reindeer are coming to drive you away
  Over the snow on an ebony sleigh
  Over the mountain and over the sea
  You shall go happy and handsome and free.

CHORUS   The future, hard to mark,
  Of a world turning in the dark,
  Where ghosts are walking and dogs bark.

MRS. RANSOM   Over the green grass pastures there
  You shall go hunting the beautiful deer,
  You shall pick flowers, the white and the blue,
  Shepherds shall flute their sweetest for you.

CHORUS   True, Love finally is great,
  Greater than all; but large the hate,
  Far larger than Man can ever estimate.

MRS. RANSOM   And in the castle tower above,
  The princess' cheek burns red for your love,
  You shall be king and queen of the land,
  Happy for ever, hand in hand.

CHORUS   But between the day and night,
  The choice is free to all, and light
  Falls equally on black and white.

(During the first verse of the chorale which follows, the light fades from the summit, so that the stage is completely darkened. Then, after a moment, the entire stage is gradually illuminated by the rising sun. The stage is empty, except for the body of RANSOM, *who lies dead on the summit of the mountain)*

HIDDEN CHORUS   Free now from indignation,
Immune from all frustration
He lies in death alone;
Now he with secret terror
And every minor error
Has also made Man's weakness known.

Whom history has deserted,
These have their power exerted,
In one convulsive throe;
With sudden drowning suction
Drew him to his destruction.
(Cresc.) But they to dissolution go.

SLOW CURTAIN

(The left-hand Stage-Box is illuminated: JAMES RANSOM, LORD STAGMANTLE, LADY ISABEL, *the* GENERAL *and* M. BLAVEK *are standing round the microphone)*

STAGMANTLE   When the aeroplane flew over F 6 and came back with the news that Ransom's body had been seen on the summit, the whole of England was plunged into mourning for one of her greatest sons; but it is a sorrow tempered with pride, that once again Englishmen have been weighed in the balance and not found wanting. Monsieur Blavek, the leader of the intrepid Ostnian climbers, will tell you how he found the bodies: I only wish to add——

JAMES   You mustn't run away with the idea that my brother was a simple person: the strong silent man of the boy's adventure story. He was very far removed from that——

BLAVEK *(with a strong accent)*   It is a great honour for me to speak to you about Mr. Ransom; and I want first to say how deeply we in Ostnia feel with you in the loss of so great a climber——

ISABEL   At this hour, the thoughts of the whole nation go out to a very brave and very lonely woman in a little South

Country cottage; already a widow and now a bereaved mother. We women who know what it means to sit at home while our neareset and dearest venture forth into unknown perils——

GENERAL   I am no climber and I never met Ransom personally; but I know courage when I see it. Ransom was a brave man and courage is the greatest quality a man can have——

JAMES   He had many sides to his character and I doubt if anyone knew the whole man. I as his brother certainly did not. He had an almost feminine sensibility which, if it had not been allied to great qualities of soul and will-power and a first class intelligence, might easily have become neurotic——

BLAVEK   Two days later, we reached the summit and found him lying there. His ice-axe lay on the rocks a little lower down——

STAGMANTLE   Exactly what happened, we shall never know——

JAMES   But, as it was, no man had a more tender conscience, was more fanatically strict with himself on questions of motive and conduct——

BLAVEK   We found the body of Gunn on the eastern arrête, about five hundred feet below the summit——

STAGMANTLE   It is probable that the bodies of Lamp and Shawcross will never be recovered; but while our thoughts are naturally centred upon their leader, their devotion to duty and their quiet heroism must never be forgotten——

JAMES   There was no sphere of human activity, whether in sport or scholarship or art, in which, if he had chosen, he could not have made supreme achievements. But he hated publicity in any form; he felt it tainted——

ISABEL   The mountain took its toll of four young lives. In the face of this terrible tragedy one is almost tempted to believe in the grim old legend of the Demon——

STAGMANTLE   Acting on his express wishes, they will bury Ransom in the quiet country churchyard of the village where he spent his childhood. And Gunn is to be laid to rest beside him——

GENERAL   He died like a soldier at his post——

BLAVEK   I am proud to have been beaten by such a man in this great climb——

STAGMANTLE   As Monsieur Blavek has said, Sport transcends all national barriers and it is some comfort to realise that this tragedy has brought two great nations closer together——

JAMES   He had all the qualities which fit a man for great office in the State, but he refused, for he dreaded the vulgarity and corruption of public life; and sometimes we poor devils who find ourselves in such positions wonder whether, perhaps, he wasn't right——

STAGMANTLE   Their names are the latest but not the least on that long roll of heroes who gave their lives for the honour of this country——
(The CURTAIN *rises. In the centre of the stage, against the cyclorama, stands a plain obelisk, on which the word* RANSOM *is engraved. The* A.*'s are standing regarding it)*

ISABEL   Freely they gave——

JAMES   They did not count the cost——

STAGMANTLE   Their name liveth for evermore——

ISABEL   They did not think of self——

GENERAL   They died for England——

JAMES   Honour——

STAGMANTLE   Service——

GENERAL   Duty——

ISABEL   Sacrifice——

STAGMANTLE   England——

BLAVEK   Ostnia——

THE OTHERS   England! England! England!
(The Stage-Box is darkened)

MR. A. *(regarding the monument with proprietary pride)*
He belongs to *us,* now!
(The CURTAIN *slowly falls)*

VINTAGE FICTION, POETRY, AND PLAYS

VINTAGE BELLES-LETTRES